The Economics of Inforn

An Introduction

The Economics of Information Technology is a concise and accessible review of some of the important economic factors affecting information technology industries. These industries are characterized by high fixed costs and low marginal costs of production, large switching costs for users, and strong network effects. These factors combine to produce some unique behavior. The book consists of the two parts. In the first part, Professor Varian outlines the basic economics of these industries. In the second part, Professors Farrell and Shapiro describe the role of intellectual property in these industries.

The clarity of the analysis and exposition makes this an ideal introduction for undergraduate and graduate students in economics, business strategy, law and related areas.

HAL R. VARIAN is the Class of 1944 Professor at the School of Information Management and Systems, the Hass School of Business, and the Department of Economics at the University of California at Berkeley.

JOSEPH FARRELL is Professor of Economics in the Department of Economics at the University of California at Berkeley. He has served as Deputy Assistant Attorney General and Chief Economist at the Anti-Trust Division, US Department of Justice, 2000–2001.

CARL SHAPIRO is the Transamerica Professor of Business Strategy at the Haas School of Business at the University of California at Berkeley. He also is Director of the Institute of Business and Economic Research, and Professor of Economics in the Economics Department at the University of California at Berkeley.

THE RAFFAELE MATTIOLI LECTURE SERIES

The Economics of Information Technology

An Introduction

Hal R. Varian
Joseph Farrell
Carl Shapiro

CAMBRIDGE
UNIVERSITY PRESS

PUBLISHED BY THE PRESS SYNDICATE OF THE UNIVERSITY OF CAMBRIDGE
The Pitt Building, Trumpington Street, Cambridge, United Kingdom

CAMBRIDGE UNIVERSITY PRESS
The Edinburgh Building, Cambridge, CB2 2RU, UK
40 West 20th Street, New York, NY 10011–4211, USA
477 Williamstown Road, Port Melbourne, VIC 3207, Australia
Ruiz de Alarcón 13, 28014 Madrid, Spain
Dock House, The Waterfront, Cape Town 8001, South Africa

http://www.cambridge.org

First published 2004

Printed in the United Kingdom at the University Press, Cambridge

Typeface Utopia 9.5/13 pt.   *System* LATEX 2$_\varepsilon$ [TB]

A catalogue record for this book is available from the British Library

Library of Congress Cataloguing in Publication data

ISBN 0 521 84415 0 hardback
ISBN 0 521 60521 0 paperback

Contents

Figures

The Raffaele Mattioli Lectures

The Raffaele Mattioli Lectures, in which many prominent economists have taken part, were established in 1976 by Banca Commerciale Italiana in association with Università Commerciale Luigi Bocconi as a memorial to the cultural legacy left by Raffaele Mattioli, for many years chairman of the bank.

Banca Commerciale Italiana then merged into Banca Intesa, which is pleased to continue promoting the new series of lectures together with Università Commerciale L. Bocconi. The aim is to create an opportunity for reflection and debate on topics of particular current interest, thus providing stimuli and ideas for the increasing challenges of a continually changing worldwide economic scenario.

The present initiative is therefore dedicated to the analysis of the effects of important changes which are now taking place in the world economy: the globalization of markets, the continuous evolution in the field of information, technology and communications and the convergence of economics and international relations.

It is evident that these changes, coupled with the European Monetary Union, provide many complex subjects that will be best dealt with from an interdisciplinary perspective.

Distinguished academics and researchers of all nationalities concerned with all kinds of economic problems will be invited to take part in this enterprise, with the intention of contributing to the debate interconnecting economic theory with practical policy.

PART ONE

Competition and market power

Hal R. Varian

1 Introduction

During the 1990s there were three back-to-back events that stimulated investment in information technology: telecommunications deregulation in 1996, the "year 2K" problem in 1998–99, and the "dot com" boom in 1999–2000. The resulting investment boom led to a dramatic run-up of stock prices for information technology companies.

Many IT companies listed their stocks on NASDAQ. Figure 1 depicts the cumulative rate of return on the NASDAQ and the S&P 500 during most of the 1990s. Note how closely the two indices track each other up until January of 1999, at which point NASDAQ took off on its roller-coaster ride. Eventually it came crashing back, but it is interesting to observe that the total return on the two markets over the eight years depicted in the figure ended up being about the same.

This is a revised version of the Raffaele Mattioli Lecture delivered at Bocconi University, Milan, Italy, on November 15–16, 2001 and the Sorbonne on March 6, 2003. It is based, in part, on the paper I delivered at the Federal Reserve Bank of Kansas City Jackson Hole Symposium, August 2001. Research support from NSF grant SES-9979852 is gratefully acknowledged, as are helpful comments by Erik Brynjolfsson, Joe Farrell, Paul Klemperer, and Kevin Murphy. Email for comments: hal@sims.berkeley.edu.

1

Cumulative Returns

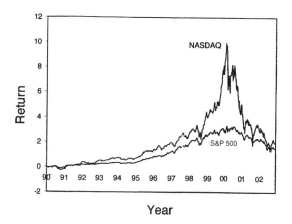

Figure 1   Return on the NASDAQ and S&P 500 during the 1990s

Figure 1 actually understates the magnitude of technology firms on stock market performance, since a significant part of the S&P return was also driven by technology stocks. In December 1990, the technology component of the S&P was only 6.5 percent; by March 2000, it was over 34 percent. By July 2001, it was about 17 percent.

A prominent Silicon Valley venture capitalist described the dramatic run-up in technology stocks as the "greatest legal creation of wealth in human history." As subsequent events showed, not all of it was legal and not all of it was wealth.

But the fact that only a few companies succeeded in capitalizing on the Internet boom does not mean that there was no social value in the investment that took place during 1999–2001. Indeed, quite the opposite is true. One can interpret figure 1 as showing something quite different from the usual interpretation, namely that competition worked very well during this period, so that much of the social gain from Internet technology ended up being passed along to consumers, leaving little surplus in the hands of investors.

Clearly the world changed dramatically in just a few short years. Email has become the communication tool of choice for many organizations. The World Wide Web, once just a scientific curiosum, has now become an indispensable tool for information workers. Instant messaging has changed the way our children communicate and is beginning to affect business communication. Many macroeconomists attribute the increase in productivity growth in the late 1990s to the investment in IT during the first half of that decade. If this is true, then it is very good news, since it suggests we have yet to reap the benefits of the IT investment of the late 1990s.[1]

2 Technology and market structure

A major focus of this monograph is the relationship between technology and market structure. High-technology industries are subject to the same market forces as every other industry. However, there are some forces that are particularly important in high-tech, and these will be our primary concern. These forces are not "new"; indeed, the forces at work in network industries in the 1990s are very similar to those that confronted the telephone and wireless industries in the 1890s.

But forces that were relatively minor in the industrial economy turn out to be critical in the information economy. Second-order effects for industrial goods are often first-order effects for information goods.

Take, for example, cost structures. Constant fixed costs and zero marginal costs are common assumptions for textbook analysis, but are rarely observed for physical products since there are capacity constraints in nearly every production process. But for information goods, this sort of cost structure is very common – indeed, it is the baseline case. This is true not just for pure information goods, but even for physical goods such as silicon chips. A chip fabrication plant can cost several billion dollars to construct and outfit, but producing an incremental chip only costs a few dollars.

---

[1] I will not address the literature on productivity in this survey; see Brynjolfsson and Hitt (2000), Steindel and Stiroh (2001), and Stiroh (2001) for an introduction to this literature. For different approaches, see Litan and Rivlin (2001) and Litan and Varian (2001).

It is rare to find cost structures this extreme outside of technology and information industries.

The effects I will discuss involve pricing, switching costs, scale economies, transactions costs, system coordination, and contracting. Each of these topics has been extensively studied in the economics literature. I do not pretend to offer a complete survey of the relevant literature, but will focus on relatively recent material in order to present a snapshot of the state of the art of research in these areas.

I try to refer to particularly significant contributions and other more comprehensive surveys. The intent is to provide an overview of the issues for an economically literate, but non-specialist, audience.

For a step up in technical complexity, I can recommend the survey of network industries in the *Journal of Economic Literature* consisting of articles by Katz and Shapiro (1994), Besen and Farrell (1994), Leibowitz and Margolis (1990), and the books by Shy (2001) and Vulkan (2003). Farrell and Klemperer (2003) contains a detailed survey of work involving switching costs and network effects with an extensive bibliography.

For a step down in technical complexity, but with much more emphasis on business strategy, I can recommend Shapiro and Varian (1998a), which contains many real-world examples.

3 Intellectual property

Information technology is used to manipulate information. Some of that information may be intellectual property. It follows that the terms and conditions of use for intellectual property play a critical role in the economics of information technology.

Copyright law defines the property rights of the product being sold. Patent law defines the conditions that affect the incentives for, and constraints on, innovation in physical devices and, increasingly, in software and business processes.

I do not directly address intellectual property issues here, but my two co-authors, Joseph Farrell and Carl Shapiro do an admirable job in part II. In addition to their contribution, I can refer the reader to the surveys by Gallini and Scotchmer (2001), Gallini (2002), and Menell (2000), and to the reviews by Shapiro (2000, 2001a). Samuelson and Varian (2002) describe some recent developments in intellectual property policy.

4 The Internet boom

First, we must confront the question of what happened during the late 1990s. Viewed from 2003, such an exercise is undoubtedly premature, and must be regarded as somewhat speculative. No doubt a clearer view will emerge as we gain better perspective on the period, but here I will offer one approach to understanding what went on.

I interpret the Internet boom of the late 1990s as an instance of what one might call "combinatorial innovation."

Every now and then a technology, or set of technologies, emerges whose rich set of components can be combined and recombined to create new products. The arrival of these components then sets off a technology boom as innovators work through the possibilities.

This is, of course, an old idea in economic history. Schumpeter (1934, p. 66) refers to "new combinations of productive means." More recently, Weitzman (1998) used the term "recombinant growth." Gilfillan (1935), Usher (1954), Kauffman (1995) and many others describe variations on essentially the same idea. The concept of "General Purpose Technologies" described in Bresnahan and Trajtenberg (1995) and Helpman (1998) is, in our terminology a particularly important type of component for combinatorial innovation.

The attempts to develop interchangeable parts during the early nineteenth century is a good example of a technology revolution driven by combinatorial innovation.[2] The gradual standardization of design of gears, pulleys, chains, cams, and other mechanical devices led to the development of the so-called "American system

---

[2] See Hounshell (1984) for the fascinating history of technological development during this period.

of manufacture" which started in the weapons manufacturing plants of New England but eventually led to a thriving industry in domestic appliances.

A century later the development of the gasoline engine led to another wave of combinatorial innovation as it was incorporated into a variety of devices from motorcycles to automobiles to airplanes.

As Schumpeter points out in several of his writings (e.g. Shumpeter, 2000), combinatorial innovation is one of the important reasons why inventions appear in waves, or "clusters," as he calls them:

> [A]s soon as the various kinds of social resistance to something that is fundamentally new and untried have been overcome, it is much easier not only to do the same thing again but also to do *similar* things in different directions, so that a first success will always produce a cluster.   (p. 142)

Schumpeter emphasizes a "demand-side" explanation for such clustering of innovation. One might also consider a complementary "supply-side" explanation: since innovators are, in many cases, working with the same components, it is not surprising to see simultaneous innovation, with several innovators coming up with essentially the same invention at almost the same time. There are many well-known examples, including the electric light, the airplane, the automobile, and the telephone.

A third explanation for waves of innovation involves the development of complements. When automobiles started to become popular in the early 1900s, where did the paved roads and gasoline engines come from? The answer: the roads were initially the result of the prior decade's bicycle boom, and gasoline was often available at the general store to fuel stationary engines used on farms. These complementary products (and others, such as pneumatic tires) were enough to get the nascent technology going; and once the growth in the automobile industry took off it stimulated further demand for roads, gasoline, oil, and other complementary products. This is an example of an "indirect network effect," which I will examine further in section 10.

The steam engine and the electrical engine also ignited rapid periods of combinatorial innovation. In the middle of the twentieth century, the integrated circuit had a huge impact on the electronics industry. Moore's law has driven the development of ever-more-powerful microelectronic devices, revolutionizing both the communications and the computer industry.

The routers that laid the groundwork for the Internet, the servers that dished up information, and the computers that individuals used to access this information were all enabled by the microprocessor.

But all of these technological revolutions took years, sometimes decades, to work themselves out. As Hounshell (1984) documents, interchangeable parts took over a century to become truly reliable. Gasoline engines took decades to develop. The microelectronics industry took thirty years to reach its current position.

But the Internet revolution took only a few years. Why was it so rapid compared to the others? One hypothesis is that the Internet revolution was minor compared to the great technological developments of the past. (See, for example, Gordon, 2000.) This may yet prove to be true – it's hard to tell at this point.

Another explanation is that the component parts of the Internet revolution were quite different from the mechanical or electrical devices that drove previous periods of combinatorial growth. The components of the Internet revolution were not physical devices at all. Instead they were "just bits." They were ideas, standards, specifications, protocols, programming languages, and software.

For such immaterial components there were no delays in manufacture, or shipping costs, or inventory problems. Unlike gears and pulleys, you can never run out of HTML! A new piece of software could be sent around the world in seconds and innovators everywhere could combine and recombine this software with other components to create a host of new applications.

Web pages, chat rooms, clickable images, web mail, MP3 files, online auctions and exchanges, blogs, wikis, . . . the list goes on and on. The important point is that all of these applications were developed from a few basic tools and protocols. They are the result of the combinatorial innovation set off by the Internet, just as the sewing machine was a result of the combinatorial innovation set off by the push for interchangeable parts in the late-eighteenth-century munitions industry.

Given the lack of physical constraints, it is no wonder that the Internet boom proceeded so rapidly. Indeed, the rapid pace of innovation continues today. As better and more powerful tools for managing and manipulating web sites have been developed, the pace of innovation has even increased, since a broader segment of the population has been able to create online software applications easily and quickly.

Twenty years ago the very idea that a loosely coupled community of programmers, with no centralized direction or authority, could develop an entire operating system would have been rejected out of hand. Such a development would have been just too absurd. But it has happened: the GNU/Linux operating system was not only created online, but has even become respectable and raised a serious threat to very powerful incumbents.

Such open-source software is like the primordial soup for combinatorial innovation. All the components are floating around in the broth, bumping up against each other and creating new molecular structures, which themselves become components for future development.

Unlike closed-source software, open source allows programmers (and "wannabe programmers") to look inside the black box to see how the applications are assembled. Such knowledge is a tremendous spur to education and innovation.

It has always been so. Look at Josephson's description of the methods of Thomas Edison:

> As he worked constantly over such machines, certain original insights came to him; by dint of many trials, materials long known to others, constructions long accepted were put together in a different way – and there you had an invention.
>
> (Josephson, 1959, p. 91)

Open source makes the inner workings of software apparent, allowing future Edisons to build on, improve, and use existing programs – combining them to create novel innovations.

One force that undoubtedly led to the very rapid expansion of the web was the fact that HTML was, by construction, open source. From conception, web browsers have enabled users to "view source," which meant that many innovations in design or functionality could immediately be adopted by imitators – and innovators – around the globe.

Perl, Python, Ruby, and other interpreted languages have the same characteristic. There is no "binary code" to hide the design of the original author. This allows subsequent users to add on to programs and systems, improving them and making them more powerful.

4.1 Financial speculation

Each of the periods of combinatorial innovation referred to in the previous section was accompanied by financial speculation. New technologies that capture the public imagination inevitably lead to an investment boom: sewing machines, the telegraph, the railroad, the automobile . . . the list could be extended indefinitely.

Perhaps the period that bears the most resemblance to the Internet boom is the so-called "Euphoria of 1923," when it was just becoming apparent that broadcast radio could be the next big thing.

The challenge with broadcast radio, as with the Internet, was how to make money from it. *Wireless World*, a hobbyist magazine, even sponsored a contest to determine the best business model for radio. The winning idea was "a tax on vacuum tubes" with radio commercials being one of the more unpopular choices.[3]

Broadcast radio, of course, set off its own stock market bubble. When the public gets excited about a new technology, a lot of "dumb money" comes into the stock market. Bubbles are a common outcome. It may be true that it's hard to start a bubble with rational investors – but not it's not that hard with real people.

Though billions of dollars were lost during the Internet bubble, a substantial fraction of the investment made during this period still has social value. Much has been made of the miles laid of

---

[3] See Smulyan (1994) for a detailed history and Hanson (1998) for a useful overview of this period.

"dark fiber." But it's just as cheap to lay 128 strands of fiber as a single strand, and the *marginal* cost of the "excess" investment is rather low.

The biggest capital investment during the bubble years was probably in human capital. The rush for financial success led to a whole generation of young adults immersing themselves in technology. Just as it was important for teenagers to know about radio during the 1920s and automobiles in the 1950s, it was important to know about computers during the 1990s. "Being digital" (whatever that meant) was clearly cool in the 1990s, just as "being mechanical" was cool in the 1950s.

This knowledge of, and facility with, computers will have large payoffs in the future. It may well be that part of the surge in productivity observed in the late 1990s came from the human capital invested in facility with spreadsheets and web pages, rather than the physical capital represented by PCs and routers. Since the hardware, the software, and the wetware – the human capital – are inexorably linked, it is almost impossible to subject this hypothesis to an econometric test.

4.2 Where are we now?

As we have seen, the confluence of Moore's law, the Internet, digital awareness, and the financial markets led to a period of rapid innovation. The result was excess capacity in virtually every dimension: compute cycles, bandwidth, and even HTML programmers. All of these things are still valuable – they're just not the source of profit that investors once thought, or hoped, that they would be.

We are now in a period of consolidation. These assets have been, and will continue to be, marked to market, to better reflect their true asset value – their potential for future earnings. This process is painful, to be sure, but not that different in principle from what happened to the automobile market or the radio market in the 1930s. We still drive automobiles and listen to the radio, and it is likely that the web – or its successor – will continue to be used in the decades to come.

The challenge now is to understand how to use the capital investment of the 1990s to improve the way that goods and services are produced. Productivity growth has accelerated during the latter part of the 1990s, and, uncharacteristically, continued to grow during the subsequent slump. Is this due to the use of information technology? Undoubtedly it played a role, though there will continue to be debates about just how important it has been.

Now we are in the quiet phase of combinatorial innovation: the components have been perfected, the initial inventions have been made, but they have not yet been fully incorporated into organizational work practices.

David (1990) has described how the productivity benefits from the electric motor took decades to reach fruition. The real breakthrough came from miniaturization and the possibility of rearranging the production process. Henry Ford, and the entire managerial team, were down on the factory floor every day fine-tuning the flow of parts through the assembly line as they perfected the process of mass production.

The challenge facing us now is to re-engineer the flow of information through the enterprise. And not only within the enterprise – the entire value chain is up for grabs. Michael Dell has shown us how direct, digital communication with the end user can be fed into production planning so as to perfect the process of "mass customization."

True, the PC is particularly susceptible to this form of organization, given that it is constructed from a relatively small set of standardized components. But Dell's example has already stimulated innovators in a variety of other industries. There are many other examples of innovative production enabled by information technology that will arise in the future.

Carr (2003, 2004) has argued that IT no longer matters, since it is now so cheap and ubiquitous that it can no longer offer a competitive advantage. He is certainly right that it is cheap and ubiquitous. But since IT is a component that is particularly suited to combinatorial innovation, it may well be that the fact that it is so cheap and ubiquitous that will stimulate further invention. To the extent that the fruits of such invention can be captured by the innovator, whether by intellectual property or by some form of first-mover advantage, there may well yet be significant competitive advantage to be had through the innovative use of IT.

4.3 The "New Economy"

There are those who claim that we need a new economics to understand the new economy of bits. I am skeptical. The old economics – or at least the old principles – work remarkably well. Many of the effects that drive the new information economy were there in the old industrial economy – you just have to know where to look.

Effects that were uncommon in the industrial economy – network effects, switching costs, and the like – are the norm in the information economy. Recent literature that aims to understand the economics of information technology is firmly grounded in the traditional literature. As with technology itself, the innovation comes not in the basic building blocks, the components of economic analysis, but rather the ways in which they are combined.

Let us turn now to this task of describing these "combinatorial innovations" in economic thinking.

5 Differentiation of products and prices

Price discrimination is important in high-tech industries for two reasons: first the high-fixed-cost, low-marginal-cost technologies commonly observed in these industries often lead to significant market power, with the usual inefficiencies. In particular, price will often exceed marginal cost, meaning that the profit benefits to price discrimination will be very apparent to the participants.

In addition, information technology allows for fine-grained observation and analysis of consumer behavior. This permits various kinds of marketing strategies that were previously extremely difficult to carry out, at least on a large scale. For example, a seller can offer prices and goods that are differentiated by individual behavior and/or characteristics.

This section will review some of the economic effects that arise from the ability to use more effective price discrimination.

5.1 First-degree price discrimination

In the most extreme case, information technology allows for a "market of one," in the sense that highly personalized products can be sold at a highly personalized price. This phenomenon is also known as "mass customization" or "personalization."

Consumers can personalize their front page at many online newspapers and portals. They can buy a personally configured computer from Dell, and even purchase computer-customized blue jeans from Levi's. We will likely see more and more possibilities for customization of both information goods and physical products.

Amazon was accused of charging different prices to different customers depending on their behavior (Rosencrance, 2000), but they claimed that this was simply market experimentation. However, the ease with which one can conduct marketing experiments on the Internet is itself notable. Presumably companies will find it much more attractive to fine-tune pricing in Internet-based commerce, eliminating the so-called "menu costs" from the pricing decision. Brynjolfsson and Smith (1999) found that Internet retailers revise their prices much more often than conventional retailers, and that prices are adjusted in much finer increments.

The theory of monopoly first-degree price discrimination is fairly simple: firms will charge the highest price they can to each consumer, thereby capturing all the consumer surplus. However, it is clear that this is an extreme case. Online sellers face competition from each other and from offline sellers, so adding competition to this textbook model is important.

Ulph and Vulkan (2000, 2001) have examined the theory of first-degree price discrimination and product differentiation in a competitive environment. In their model, consumers differ with respect to the products they find most desirable, and firms choose where to locate in product space and how much to charge each consumer. Ulph and Vulkan find that there are two significant effects: the "enhanced surplus extraction effect" and the "intensified competition effect." The first effect refers to the fact that personalized pricing allows firms to charge prices closer to the reservation price for each consumer; the second effect refers to the fact that each consumer is a market to be contested. In one model they find that when consumer tastes are not dramatically different, the intensified competition effect dominates the surplus extraction effect, making firms worse off and consumers better off with competitive personalized pricing than with nonpersonalized pricing.

This is an interesting result, but their model assumes full information. Thus it leaves out the possibility that long-time suppliers of consumers know more about their customers than alternative suppliers. Sellers place much emphasis on "owning the consumer." An extended relationship allows the seller to understand "their" consumers' purchasing habits and needs better than potential competitors. Amazon's personalized recommendation service works well for me, since I have bought books there in the past. A new seller would not have this extensive experience with my purchase history, and would therefore offer me inferior service.

Of course, I could search on Amazon and purchase elsewhere, but there are other cases where free riding of this sort is not feasible. For example, a company called AmeriServe provides paper supplies to fast-food stores. As a by-product, they found that their records about customer orders allowed them to provide better analysis and forecasts of their customers' needs than could the customers themselves. Due to this superior information, AmeriServe was able to offer services to their customers such as recommended orders for restock. Such services were valuable to AmeriServe's customers, and therefore gave it an edge over competitive suppliers, allowing it to charge a premium for providing this service, either via a flat fee or via higher prices for their products.

Personalized pricing obviously raises privacy issues. A seller that knows its customers' tastes can sell them products that fit their needs better but it will also be able to charge more for the superior service.

Obviously, I may want my tailor, my doctor, and my accountant to understand my needs and provide me with customized services. However, it is equally obvious that I do not, in general, want them to share this information with third parties, at least without my consent. The issue is not privacy per se, but rather trust: consumers want to control how information about themselves is used.

In economic terms, bilateral contracts involving personal information can be used to enhance efficiency, at least when transactions costs are low. But sale of information to third parties, without consumer consent, would not involve explicit contracting, and there is no reason to think it would be efficient. What is needed, presumably, are default contracts to govern markets in personal information. The optimal structure of these default contracts will depend on the nature of the transactions costs associated with various arrangements. I discuss these issues in more detail in Varian (1997).

Another issue relating to personalized pricing and mass customization is advertising. Many of the services that use personalization also rely heavily on revenue from advertising. Internet search engines, for example, charge significantly more for ads keyed to "hot words" in search queries since these ads are being shown to consumers who may find them particularly relevant. Google currently has well over 100,000 advertisers who bid on keywords and phrases. When a user searches for information that is related to these keywords Google shows relevant ads. The bids, along with other information such as past clickthrough rates, affect how the ads are displayed.

5.2 Second-degree price discrimination

Second-degree price discrimination refers to a situation where everyone faces the same menu of prices for a set of related products. It is also known as "product line pricing," "market segmentation," or "versioning." The idea is that sellers use their knowledge of the *distribution* of consumer tastes to design a product line that appeals to different market segments.

This form of price discrimination is, of course, widely used. Automobiles, consumer electronics, and many other products are commonly sold in product lines. We don't normally think of information goods as being sold in product lines but, upon reflection, it can be seen that this is a common practice. Books are available in hardback or paperback, in libraries, and for purchase. Movies are available in theaters, on airplanes, on tape, on DVD, and on TV. Newspapers are available online and in physical form. Traditional information goods are very commonly sold in different versions.

Information versioning has also been adopted on the Internet. To choose just one example, 20-minute delayed stock prices are available on Yahoo free of charge, but real-time stock quotes cost $9.95 a month. In this case, the providers are using "delay" to version their information.

Information technology is helpful in both collecting information about consumers, to help design product lines, and in actually producing the different versions of the product itself. See Shapiro and Varian (1998a, 1998b), and Varian (2001) for an analysis of versioning.

The basic problem in designing a product line is "competing against yourself." Often consumers with high willingness to pay will be attracted by lower-priced products that are targeted towards consumers with less willingness to pay. This "self-selection problem" can be solved by lowering the price of the high-end products, by lowering the "quality" of the low-end products, or by some combination of the two.

Making the quality adjustments may be worthwhile even when it is costly, raising the peculiar possibility that the low-end products may be costly to produce than the high-end products. See Deneckere and McAfee (1996) for a general treatment and Shapiro and Varian (1998a) for applications in the information goods context.

Varian (2001) analyzes some of the welfare consequences of versioning. Roughly speaking, versioning is good in that it allows markets to be served that would otherwise not be served. This is the standard output-enhancing effect of price discrimination described in Schmalensee (1981b) and Varian (1985). However, the social cost of versioning is the quality reduction necessary to satisfy the self-selection constraint. In many cases the output effect appears to outweigh the quality reduction effect, suggesting that versioning is often welfare-enhancing.

Versioning is being widely adopted in the technology-intensive information goods industry. Intuit sells three different versions of their home accounting and tax software, Microsoft sells a number of versions of its operating systems and applications software, and even Hollywood has learned how to segment audiences for home video. The latest trend in DVDs is to sell a "standard" version for one price and an enhanced "collector's edition" for five or ten dollars more. The more elaborate version contains outtakes, director's commentary, storyboards and the like. This gives the studios a way to price discriminate between collectors and casual viewers, and between buyers and renters. Needless to say, the price differences between the two versions is much greater than the difference in marginal cost.

5.3 Third-degree price discrimination

Third-degree price discrimination is selling at different prices to different groups. It is, of course, a classic form of price discrimination and is widely used.

The conventional treatment examines monopoly price discrimination, but there have been some recent attempts to extend this analysis to the competitive case. Armstrong and Vickers (2001) present a survey of this literature, along with a unified treatment and a number of new results. In particular they observe that when consumers have essentially the same tastes, and there is a fixed cost of servicing each consumer, then competitive third-degree price discrimination will generally make consumers better off. The reason is that competition forces firms to maximize consumer utility, and price discrimination gives them additional flexibility in dealing with the fixed cost. If there are no fixed costs, consumer utility falls with competitive third-degree price discrimination, even though overall welfare (consumer plus producer surplus) will still rise.

With heterogeneous consumers, the situation is not as clear. Generally consumer surplus is reduced and profits are enhanced by competitive price discrimination, so welfare may easily fall.

5.4 Conditioning on purchase history

Another form of price discrimination that is of considerable interest in high-tech markets is price discrimination based on purchase history. Fudenberg and Tirole (1998) investigate models where a monopolist can discriminate between old and new customers by offering upgrades, enhancements, and the like. Fudenberg and Tirole (2000) investigate a duopoly model which adds an additional phenomenon of "poaching": one firm can offer a low-ball price to steal another's customers. These results are extended by Villas-Boas (1999, 2001).

Acquisti and Varian (2001) examine a simple model with two types of consumers, high-value and low-value, in which a monopolist can commit to a price plan. They find that although a monopolistic seller is able to make offers conditional on previous purchase history, it is never profitable for it to do so, which is consistent with the earlier analysis of intertemporal price discrimination by Stokey (1979) and Salant (1989).

However, Acquisti and Varian (2001) also show that if the monopolist can offer an enhanced service such as one-click shopping or recommendations based on purchase history, it may be optimal to condition prices on earlier behavior and extract some of the value from this enhanced service.

Even in a competitive environment, a seller may have a partial monopoly in providing personalized services since it can customize those services in light of previously observed purchase behavior. The resulting equilibrium exhibits a form of lock-in: some of the consumers are loyal to the vendors they originally patronized, since those vendors are able to provide personalized enhanced services that they find particularly valuable.

5.5 Search

One interesting effect of the Internet is that it can lower the cost of search quite dramatically. Even in markets where there are relatively few direct online transactions, such as automobile sales, consumers appear to do quite a bit of information gathering before purchase.

There are many shopping agents that allow for easy price comparisons. According to Yahoo, mySimon, BizRate, PriceScan, and DealTime are among the most popular of these services. What happens when some of the consumers use shopping agents and others shop at random? This question has been addressed by Greenwald and Kephart (1999), Baye and Morgan (2001), Baye, Morgan, and Scholten (2001) and others. The structure of the problem is similar to that of Varian (1980), and it is not surprising that the solution is the same: sellers want to use a mixed strategy and randomize the prices they charge. This allows them to sometimes charge low prices so as to compete for the searchers and still charge, on average, a high price to the non-searchers. In my 1980 paper I interpreted this randomization as promotional sales; in the Internet context it is better seen as small day-to-day fluctuations in price. Baye et al. (2001) and Brynjolfsson and Smith (1999) show that online firms do engage in frequent small price adjustments, similar to those predicted by the theory. Janssen and Moraga-González (2001) examine how the equilibrium changes as the intensity of search changes in this sort of model.

One reason that more people don't use "shopbots" may be that they do not trust the results. Ellison and Ellison (2001) have found that it is common for online retailers to engage in "bait and switch" tactics: they will advertise an inferior version of a product (e.g. an obsolete memory chip) in order to attract users to their site. Such obfuscation may discourage users from shopbots, leading to the kind of price discrimination described above.

5.6 Bundling

Bundling refers to the practice of selling two or more distinct goods together for a single price (Adams and Yellen, 1976). This is particularly attractive for information goods since the marginal cost of adding an extra good to a bundle is negligible. There are two distinct economic effects involved: reduced dispersion of willingness to pay, which is a form of price discrimination, and increased barriers to entry, which is a separate issue.

To see how the price dispersion story works, consider a software producer who sells both a word processor and a spreadsheet. Mark is willing to pay $120 for the word processor and $100 for the spreadsheet. Noah is willing to pay $100 for the word processor and $120 for the spreadsheet.

If the vendor is restricted to a uniform price, it will set a price of $100 for each software product, realizing revenue of $400.

But suppose the vendor bundles the products into an "office suite." If the willingness to pay for the bundle is the sum of the willingness to pay for the components, then each consumer will be willing to pay $220 for the bundle, yielding a revenue of $440 for the seller.

The enhanced revenue is due to the fact that bundling has reduced the dispersion of willingness to pay: essentially it has made the demand curve flatter. This example is constructed so that the willingnesses to pay are negatively correlated, thus the reduction is especially pronounced. But the law of large numbers tells us that unless a number of random variables are *perfectly* correlated, summing them up will tend to reduce relative dispersion, making the demand curve more elastic.

Bakos and Brynjolfsson (1999, 2000, 2001) have explored this issue in considerable detail and show that bundling significantly enhances firm profit and overall efficiency, but at the cost of a reduction in consumer surplus. They also note that these effects are much stronger for information goods than for physical goods, due to the zero marginal cost of information goods.

Armstrong (1999) works in a somewhat more general model which allows for correlated tastes. He finds that an "almost optimal" pricing system can be implemented as a menu of two-part tariffs, with the variable part of the pricing proportional to marginal costs.

Whinston (1990), Nalebuff (1999, 2000) and Bakos and Brynjolfsson (2000) examine the entry deterrent effect of bundling. To continue with the office suite example, consider a more general situation where there are many consumers with different valuations for word processors and spreadsheets. By selling a bundled office suite, the monopoly software vendor reaches many of those who value both products highly and some of those who value only one of the products highly.

If a competitor contemplates entering either market, it will see that its most attractive customers are already taken. Thus it finds that the residual demand for its product is much reduced – making entry a much less attractive strategy. In many cases the only way a potential entry could effectively compete would be to offer a bundle with both products. This not only increases development costs dramatically, but it also makes competition very intense in the suite market – a not so sweet outcome for the entrant. When Sun decided to enter the office suite market with StarOffice, a competitor for Microsoft Office, it offered the package at a price of zero, recognizing that it would take such a dramatic price to make headway against Microsoft's imposing lead.

6 Switching costs and lock-in

When you switch automobiles from Ford to GM, the change is relatively painless. If you switch from Windows to Linux, it can be very costly. You may have to change document formats, applications software, and, most importantly, you will have to invest substantial time and effort in learning the new operating environment.

Changing software environments at the organizational level is also very costly. One study found that the total cost of installing an Enterprise Resource Planning (ERP) system such as SAP was eleven times greater than the purchase price of the software due to the cost of infrastructure upgrades, consultants, retraining programs, and the like.

These switching costs are endemic in high-technology industries and can be so large that switching suppliers is virtually unthinkable, a situation known as "lock-in."

Switching costs and lock-in has been extensively studied in the economics literature. See, for example, Klemperer (1987, 1995), Farrell and Shapiro (1988, 1989), and Beggs and Klemperer (1992). The last work is a particularly useful survey of earlier work. Shapiro and Varian (1998a) examine some of the business strategy implications of switching costs and lock-in.

6.1 Simple analytics of lock-in

Consider the following simple two-period model, adopted from Klemperer (1995). There are n consumers, each of whom is willing to pay v per period to buy a non-durable good. There are two producers that produce the good at a constant identical marginal cost of c. The producers are unable to commit to future prices.

In order to switch consumption from one firm to the other, a consumer must pay a switching cost s. We suppose $v \geq c$, but $v + s < c$, so that it pays each consumer to purchase the good but not to switch.

The unique Nash equilibrium in the second period is for each firm to set its price to the monopoly price v, making profit of $v - c$. The seller can extract full monopoly profit in the second period, since the consumers are "locked-in," meaning that their switching costs are so high that the competitive seller is unable to offer them a price sufficiently low to induce them to switch.

The determination of the first-period price will be discussed below, after we consider a few real-world examples.

6.2 Competition to acquire customers

When switching costs are significantly high, competition can be intense to attract new customers, since, once they are locked in, they can be a substantial source of profit. Everyone has had the experience of buying a nice, cheap inkjet only to discover a few months later that the price of replacement cartridges is almost half the cost of the printer. The notable fact is not that the cartridges are expensive, but rather that the printer is so cheap. And, of course, the printer is so cheap *because* the cartridges are so expensive. The printer manufacturers are following the time-tested strategy of giving away the razor to sell the blades.

Business Week reports that in 2000, HP's printer supply division made an estimated $500 million in operating profit on sales of $2.4 billion. The rest of HP's businesses lost $100 million on revenues of $9.2 billion. The inkjet cartridges reportedly have over 50 percent profit margins (Roman, 2001).

In a related story, Cowell (2001) reports that SAP's profits rose by 78 percent in the second-quarter of 2001, even in the midst of a widespread technology slump. As he explains, "because SAP has some 14,000 existing customers using its products, it is able to sell them updated Internet software . . .".

Ausubel (1991) and Kim, Kliger, and Vale (2003) examine switching costs in the credit card and bank loan markets and find that they are substantial: in the bank loan case, they appear to amount to about a third of the average interest rate on loans.

Chen and Hitt (2001) use a random utility model to study switching costs for online brokerage firms. They find that breadth of product offering is the single best explanatory variable in their model, and that demographic variables are not very useful predictors. This is important since breadth of product offerings is under control of the firm; if a variety of products can be offered at a reasonable cost, then it should help in reducing the likelihood of customer switching.

As these examples illustrate, lock-in can be very profitable for firms. It is not obvious that switching costs necessarily reduce consumer welfare, since the competition to acquire the customers can be quite beneficial to consumers. For example, consumers who use their printers much less than average are clearly made better off by having a low price for printers, even though they have to pay a high price for cartridges.

The situation may be somewhat different for companies like SAP, Microsoft, or Oracle. They suffer from the "burden of the locked-in customers," in the sense that they would like to sell at a high price to their current customers (on account of their switching costs) but would also like to compete aggressively for new customers, since they will remain customers for a long time and contribute to future profit flows. This naturally leads such firms to want to price discriminate in favor of new customers, and such strategies are commonly used.

Though he acknowledges that in many cases welfare may go either way, Klemperer (1995) concludes that switching costs are generally bad for consumer welfare: they typically raise prices over the lifetime of the product, create deadweight loss, and reduce entry.

6.3 Analytics of competition to acquire customers

Return to the model of section 6.1. Suppose for simplicity that the discount rate is zero, so that the sellers care only about the sum of the profit over the two periods. In this case, each firm would be willing to pay up to $v - c$ to acquire a customer.

Bertrand competition pushes the present value of the profit of each firm to zero, yielding a first period price of $2c - v$. The higher the second-period monopoly payoff, the smaller the first-period price will be, reflecting the result of the competition to acquire the monopoly.

If we assumed the goods were partial substitutes, rather than perfect substitutes, we would get a less extreme result, but it is still typically the case that the first-period price is lower because of the second-period lock-in. See Klemperer (1989, 1995) for a detailed analysis of this point.

It is worth noting that the conclusion that first-period prices are lower due to switching costs depends heavily on the assumption that the sellers cannot commit to second-period prices. If the sellers *can* commit to second-period prices, the model collapses to a one-period model, where the usual Bertrand result holds. In the specific model discussed here, the price for two periods of consumption would be competed down to $2c$.

6.4 Switching costs and price discrimination

One common example of switching costs involves specialized supplies, as with inkjet printer cartridges. In this example, the switching cost is the purchase of a new printer. The market is competitive *ex ante*, but since cartridges are incompatible, it is monopolized *ex post*.

This situation can also be viewed as a form of price discrimination. The consumer cares about the price of the printer plus the price of however many cartridges he or she buys. If all consumers are identical, a monopolist that commits to future prices would set the price of the cartridges equal to their marginal cost and use its monopoly power on the printer. This is just the two-part tariff result of Oi (1971) and Schmalensee (1981a).

Suppose now that there are two types of customers, those with high demand and those with low demand. Let p be the price of cartridges, c their marginal cost, $x_H(p)$ be the demand function of the high-demand type and $x_L(p)$ the demand of the low-demand type. Let $v_L(p)$ be the indirect utility of the low-demand type. Then the profit maximization problem for the monopolist is

$$\max_p 2v_L(p) + (p-c)[x_H(p) + x_L(p)].$$

Recalling that $v'_L(p) = -x_L(p)$, we can write the first-order conditions as:

$$p - c = \frac{x_L(p) - x_H(p)}{x'_L(p) + x'_H(p)}.$$

Hence the greater the gap between the high demand and the low demand, the larger the price-cost margin.

What is happening here is that the users distinguish their type by the amount of their usage, so the seller can price discriminate by building in a positive price-cost margin on the usage rather than the initial purchase price.

7 Supply-side economies of scale

We have already noted that many information- and technology-related businesses have cost structures with large fixed costs and small, or even zero, marginal costs. They are, to use the textbook term, "natural monopolies." The solution to natural monopolies offered in many textbooks is government regulation. But regulation offers its own inefficiencies, and there are several reasons why the social loss from high-fixed-cost, low-marginal-cost industries may be substantially less than is commonly believed.

First, competition in the real world is much more dynamic than in the textbook examples. The textbook analysis starts with the existence of a monopoly, but rarely does it examine how that monopoly came about.

Second, if the biggest firm has the most significant cost advantages, firms will compete intensively to be biggest, and consumers will benefit from that competition, as described in section 6.2. Amazon believed, rightly or wrongly, that scale economies were very important in online retailing, and consumers benefited from the low prices it charged while it was trying to build market share.

Third, information technology has reduced fixed costs and thus the minimum efficient scale of operation in many markets. Typography and page layout used to be tasks that only experts could carry out; now anyone with a mid-range computer can accomplish reasonably professional layout. Desktop publishing has led to an explosion of new entrants in the magazine business. (Of course, it is also true that many of these entrants have been subsequently acquired due to other economies of scope and scale in the industry; see Kuczynski, 2001.)

The same thing will happen to other content industries, such as movie making, where digital video offers very substantial cost reductions and demand for variety is high.

Even chip making may be vulnerable: researchers are now using off-the-shelf inkjet printers to print integrated circuits on metallic film, a process that could dramatically change the economics of this industry.

When costs are falling rapidly, and the market is growing rapidly, it is often possible to overcome cost advantages via leapfrogging. Even though the largest firm may have a cost advantage at any point in time, if the market is growing at 40 percent per year, the tables can be turned very rapidly. Wordstar and Wordperfect once dominated the word processor market; Visicalc and Lotus once dominated the spreadsheet market. Market share alone is no guarantee of success.

Christensen (1997) has emphasized the role of "disruptive technologies": low-cost, and, initially low-quality, innovations that unseat established industry players. Examples are RAID arrays of disk drives, low-cost copiers, inkjet printers, and similar developments. Just as nature abhors a vacuum, inventors and entrepreneurs abhor a monopoly, and invest heavily in trying to invent around the blocking technology. Such investment may be deadweight loss, but it may sometimes lead to serendipitous discoveries.

For example, much money was spent trying to invent around the xerography patents. One outcome was inkjet printers. These never really competed very well with black and white xerography, but have become dramatically more cost-effective technologies than xerography for color printing.

Fourth, it should also be remembered that many declining average cost industries involve durables of one form or another. PCs and operating systems are technologically obsolete far before they are functionally obsolete. In these industries the installed base creates formidable competition for suppliers since the sellers continually have to convince their users to upgrade. The "durable goods monopoly" literature inspired by Coase (1972) is not just a theoretical curiosum, but is rather a topic of intense concern in San Jose and Redmond.

Finally, we should mention the pressures on price from producers of complementary products. Since the cost of an information system to the end user depends on the sum of the prices of the components, each component maker would like to see low prices for the *other* components. Hardware makers want cheap software and vice versa. I explore this in more depth in section 10.

In summary, although supply-side economies of scale may lead to more concentrated industries, this may not be so bad for consumers as is often thought. Price discipline still asserts itself through at least four different routes:

> *Competition to acquire monopoly* In many cases the competition to acquire a monopoly will force lower prices for consumers, at least for a time. However, such competition may also produce inefficient rent dissipation, as described in Fudenberg and Tirole (1985, 1987), Hillman and Riley (1989), and below.
>
> *Reduction in fixed costs* IT has, in many cases, tended to reduce fixed costs over time, leading to more entrants, particularly in industries where there is high demand for variety. Even in commodity industries, rapid reduction in costs and rapidly growing markets offer a fertile ground for competition and disruptive technologies.
>
> *Competition with your prior production* Often, the installed base of a firm's own output is a formidable competitor, particularly when technological progress is so rapid as to exceed the ability to utilize technology fully.

Pressure from complementors Sellers of complementary products want to see lower system prices, and have various ways to exert pressure to accomplish this. This sort of "co-opetition" can be a very powerful force. Brandenburger and Nalebuff (1996) have explored several ramifications; I discuss this further in section 10.

7.1 Competition and welfare

Despite these four effects, there is still a presumption that in a mature industry that exhibits large fixed costs, equilibrium price will typically exceed marginal cost, leading to the conventional inefficiencies. See Delong and Froomkin (2001) for an extended discussion of this issue.

However, it should be remembered that, even in a static model, the correct formulation for the efficiency condition is that *marginal* price should equal marginal cost. If the information good (or chip, or whatever) is sold to different consumers at different prices, profit seeking behavior may well result in an outcome where users with low willingnesses to pay may end up facing very low prices, implying that efficiency losses are not substantial.

The traditional view of monopoly is that it creates deadweight loss and producer surplus, labeled DW and PS in figure 2a. However, perfect price discrimination eliminates the deadweight loss and competition for the monopoly transfers the resulting monopoly rents to the consumers, as shown in figure 2b.

The first and second theorems of welfare economics assert that (1) a competitive equilibrium is Pareto efficient, and (2) under certain convexity assumptions every Pareto efficient outcome can be supported as a competitive equilibrium. Under conditions of high fixed cost and low marginal cost, it is well known that a competitive equilibrium may not exist, so the first theorem is irrelevant, and the required convexity conditions may not hold, making the second welfare theorem also irrelevant.

But figure 2b suggestions what we might call the third and fourth theorems of welfare economics: (3) a perfectly discriminating monopolist can capture all surplus for itself and therefore produce Pareto efficient output, and (4) competition among

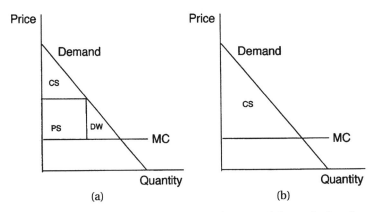

Figure 2 Competition for an (a) ordinary and (b) perfectly price discriminating monopolist

perfectly discriminating monopolists will transfer this surplus to consumers, yielding the same outcome as pure competition. These are, of course, standard observations in any intermediate microeconomics text. However, surprisingly little attention has been paid to them in the more advanced literature.

These "theorems" have not been precisely stated, although it is clearly possible to write down simple models where they hold. In reality, price discrimination is never perfect and competition for monopoly is never costless. But then again, the assumptions for the first and second welfare theorems are not exactly satisfied in reality either.

As with the first and second welfare theorems, the third and fourth welfare theorems should be viewed as parables: under certain conditions market forces may have desirable outcomes. In particular, one should not necessarily assume that large returns to scale will necessarily result in reduced consumer welfare, particularly in environments where price discrimination is possible and competition is intense.

7.2 Competing for monopoly

Even in the ideal world depicted in figure 2, two important qualifications must be kept in mind. The first has to do with the choice of the dimensions in which to compete, the second has to do with the rules of competition.

7.2.1 THE CURRENCY OF COMPETITION

The fourth welfare theorem assumes that the competition for the monopoly rent necessarily benefits consumers. If the strategic variables for the firms are prices, this is probably true. Other strategic choices such as innovation, quality choice, and so on also tend to benefit consumers. However, firms may also compete on other dimensions that have less benign consequences, such as political lobbying, the accumulation of excess capacity, and premature entry.

There is a large literature on each of these topics. One defect with the typical approach of this literature is its assumption that there is a single dimension to competition between firms: bribes to bureaucrats, prices to consumers, quality choice, entry timing, and so on. In reality, there may be many dimensions to competition, some of which are transfer payments to consumers (such as prices), some of which are transfers to third parties (such as bribes), and some of which involve pure rent dissipation (such as investment in capacity that is never used). All of these dimensions may be used simultaneously.

I believe that the choice of dimensions in which to compete has not received sufficient attention in the literature and that this is a fruitful area for future research. It also has considerable relevance for competition policy. From the viewpoint of competing for a monopoly, promotional pricing or the adoption of inferior technology are both costs to the firms, but they may have very important differences for consumer welfare calculations. Designing an environment in which competition results in transfers to consumers, rather than wasteful rent dissipation, is clearly an attractive policy goal.

For example, suppose that there is a resource that confers some sort of monopoly power. It may make more sense for the government to auction off this resource than to allow firms to compete for it using more wasteful currencies such as political lobbying. This, of course, has been part of the rationale for various privatization efforts in recent decades, but the lesson is more general. Another important example is compulsory licensing of intellectual property which may be attractive if there are high transactions costs to bargaining.

Competition is generally a good thing, but some regulation may be required to make sure that competition takes socially beneficial forms. The goal of a footrace is to see who can run the fastest, not who is the most adept at tripping their opponents or rigging the clock.

7.2.2 RULES OF THE GAME

Even if the currency of competition does not involve excessive waste, the form that competition takes – the rules of the game – can be critical in determining how much of the prize – the value of the monopoly – gets passed along to consumers.

A useful way to model this is to think of the monopoly as a prize to be auctioned off. Different auction forms describe different forms of competition.

Consider, for example, two makers of Enterprise Resource Planning (ERP) systems who are bidding to install their systems in Fortune 500 companies. This might reasonably be modeled as an *English auction*, in which the highest bidder gets the monopoly, but pays the second-highest bid. If the two bidders have different costs, but are selling an identical product, the winning bidder still retains some surplus.

Alternatively, we could imagine an *everyone pays auction*, such as a patent race or a race to build scale. In these cases, each party has to pay, and we might assume that the party who pays the most wins the monopoly.

Let v_1 be the value of the prize (the monopoly) to player 1 and v_2 the value to player 2, which we assume to be common knowledge. When the players are symmetric, so $v_1 = v_2$, the sum of the payments by the players equals the expected value of the prize.

When players are not symmetric, the equilibrium has a more interesting structure. The player with the highest value always bids for the monopoly; but the player with the second-highest value will bid only with probability v_2/v_1. If v_2 is small relatively to v_1, then the equilibrium expected payment approaches $v_2/2$, which is half the payment in the English auction. (See Hillman and Riley, 1989, for a thorough analysis of this game and Riley, 1999, for a summary.)

The difference arises because in the equilibrium strategy the player with a very low value for the monopoly often doesn't bid at all. This induces the player with the high value to shave its bid, resulting in lower auction revenues which, in our context, translate to consumers ending up with less surplus.

Yet a third example is a *war of attrition* in which both players compete until one drops out. Riley (1999) analyzes this game in some detail and shows that there is a continuum of equilibrium strategies. He presents an equilibrium selection argument that chooses an equilibrium where the player with the lower value drops out immediately. In this case, the player with the highest value for the monopoly wins the monopoly without having to compete at all!

Think, for example, of two firms that contemplate pricing below cost in order to build market share, as in a lock-in model. One firm is known to value the monopoly much more than the other, perhaps due to significantly lower production costs. In this case, it is not implausible that the firm with a lower value would give up at the outset, realizing that it would not be able to compete effectively against the other.

This could be a great deal for the winning firm – and a bad deal for the consumers since they do not benefit from the competition for the eventual monopoly.

The lesson from the "everyone pays auction" and the "war of attrition" is that if all parties have to pay to compete, you may end up with less competition and therefore fewer benefits passed along to consumers. An auction where only the winner pays is much better from the social point of view.

Clearly, many different models of competition are possible, with different models having different implications for how the surplus is divided between consumers and firms competing for the monopoly. I've sketched out some of the possibilities, but there are many other variations (e.g. contestable markets) and I expect that this is a promising area for future research.

One final point is worth making. I have already observed that under certain conditions, the competition to acquire a price discriminating monopoly will dissipate all rents. If the dissipation involves offering heavy discounts to consumers, for example, then the gain in surplus that consumers receive in the competition phase may offset, at least to some degree, the losses incurred in the monopoly phase, as in the lock-in model described earlier.

But there is clearly a time consistency problem here. Even in the ideal circumstances of the fourth welfare theorem, gains that accrue to early generations may not affect the acquiescence of later generations to monopoly power. The fact that my father got a great deal on Lotus 123 or Wordperfect may be of little solace to me when I have to pay a high price for their successors.

8 Demand-side economies of scale

Demand-side economies of scale are also known as "network externalities" or "network effects," since they commonly occur in network industries. Formally, a good exhibits network effects if the demand for the good depends on how many other people purchase it. The classic example is a fax machine; picture phones and email exhibit the same characteristic.

The literature distinguishes between "direct network effects," of the sort just described, and "indirect network effects," which are sometimes known as "chicken and egg problems." I don't directly care whether or not you have a DVD player – that doesn't affect the value of my DVD player. However, the more people that have DVDs, the more DVD-readable content will be provided, which I do care about. So, indirectly, your DVD player purchase tends to enhance the value of my player.

Indirect network effects are endemic in high-tech products. Current challenges include residential broadband and applications, and 3G wireless and applications. In each case, the demand for the infrastructure depends on the availability of applications, and vice versa. The cure for the current slump, according to industry pundits, is a new killer app. Movies on demand, interactive TV, mobile commerce – there are plenty of candidates, but investors are wary, and for good reason: there are very substantial risks involved.

I will discuss the indirect network effects in section 10. In this section, I focus on the direct case.

I like to use the terminology "demand-side economies of scale" since it forms a nice parallel with the classic supply-side economies of scale discussed in the previous section. With supply-side economies, average cost decreases with scale, while with demand-side economies of scale, average revenue (demand) increases with scale. Much of the discussion in the previous section about competition to acquire a monopoly also applies in the case of demand-side economies of scale.

When network effects are present, there are normally multiple equilibria. If no one adopts a network good, then it has no value, so no one wants it. If there are enough adopters, then the good becomes valuable, so more adopt it – making it even more valuable. Hence network effects give rise to positive feedback.

We can depict this process in a simple supply–demand diagram. The demand curve (or, more precisely, the "fulfilled expectations demand curve") for a network good typically exhibits the hump shape depicted in figure 3. As the number of adopters increases, the marginal willingness to pay for the good also increases due to the network externality; eventually, the demand curve starts to decline due to the usual effects of selling to consumers with progressively lower willingness to pay.

In the case depicted, with a perfectly elastic supply curve, there are three equilibria. Under the natural dynamics, which has quantity sold increasing when demand is greater than supply and decreasing when demand is less than supply, the two extreme equilibria are stable and the middle equilibrium is unstable.

Hence the middle equilibrium represents the "critical mass." If the market can get above this critical mass, the positive feedback kicks in and the product zooms off to success. But if the product never reaches a critical mass of adoption, it is doomed to fall back to the stable zero-demand/zero-supply equilibrium.

Consider an industry where the price of the product – a fax machine, say – is very high, but is gradually reduced over time.

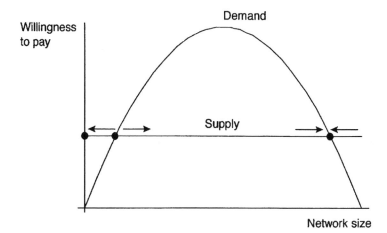

Figure 3   Demand and supply for a network good

As figure 3 shows, the critical mass will then become smaller and smaller. Eventually, due to random fluctuation or due to a deliberate strategy, the sales of the product will exceed the critical mass. Though this story is evocative, I must admit that the dynamics is rather ad hoc. It would be nice to have a more systematic derivation of dynamics in network industries. Unfortunately, microeconomic theory is notoriously weak when it comes to dynamics and there is not very much empirical work to determine with certainty what dynamic specifications make sense. The problem is that for most network goods, the frequency of data collection is too low to capture the interesting dynamics.

Figure 4 depicts the prices and shipments of fax machines in the US during the 1980s. Note the dramatic drop in price and the contemporaneous dramatic increase in demand in the middle of the decade. This is certainly consistent with the story told above, but it is hardly conclusive. Economides and Himmelberg (1995) make an attempt to estimate a model based on these data, but, as they acknowledge, this is quite difficult to do with low-frequency time-series data.

There have been some attempts to empirically examine network models using cross sectional data. Goolsbee and Klenow (2000) examine the diffusion of home computers and find a significant effect for the influence of friends and neighbors in

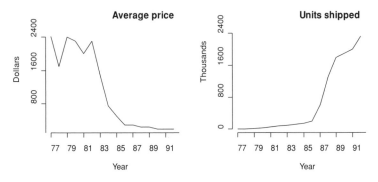

Figure 4   Price and shipments of fax machines

computer purchase decisions, even when controlling for other income, price, and demographic effects.

All these examples refer to network externalities for a competitive industry selling a compatible product: a fax machine, email, or similar product. Rohlfs (1974) was the first to analyze this case in the economics literature; he was motivated by AT&T's disastrous introduction of the PicturePhone.

Katz and Shapiro (1985, 1986a, 1986b, 1992) have examined the impact of network externalities in oligopoly models in which technology adoption is a key strategic variable. Economides (1996) and Katz and Shapiro (1994) provide useful reviews of the literature, while Rohlfs (2001) provides a history of industries in which network effects played a significant role.

Network effects are clearly prominent in some high-technology industries. Think, for example, of office productivity software such as word processors. If you are contemplating learning how to use a word processor, it is natural to lean towards the one with the largest market share, since that will make it easy to exchange files with other users, easier to work on multi-authored documents, and easy to find help if you encounter a problem. If you are choosing an operating system, it is natural to choose the one that has the most applications of interest to you. Here the applications exhibit direct network effects and the operating system/applications together exhibit indirect network effects.

Since many forms of software also exhibit supply-side increasing returns to scale, the positive feedback can be particularly strong: more sales lead to both lower unit costs and greater appeal to new customers. Once a firm has established market dominance with a particular product, it can be extremely hard to unseat it. In the context of the Microsoft antitrust case, this effect is known as the "applications barrier to entry." See Gilbert and Katz (2001), Klein (2001), and Whinston (2001) for an analysis of some of these concepts in that context.

Network effects are also related to two of the forces I described earlier: price discrimination and lock-in.

When network effects are present, early adopters may value the network good less than subsequent adopters. Thus, it makes sense for sellers to offer them a lower price, a practice known as "penetration pricing" in this context.

Network effects also contribute to lock-in. The more people that drive on the right-hand side of the road, the more valuable it is to me to follow suit. Conversely, a decision to drive on the left-hand side of the road is most effective if everyone does it at the same time. In this case, the switching costs are due to the cost of coordination among millions of individuals, a cost that may be extremely large.

9 Standards

If the value of a network depends on its size, then interconnection and/or standardization becomes an important strategic decision.

Generally, dominant firms with established networks or proprietary standards prefer not to interconnect. In the 1890s the Bell System refused to allow access to its new long-distance service to any competing carriers. In 1900–1912 Marconi International Marine Corporation licensed equipment, but wouldn't sell it, and refused to interconnect with other systems. In 1910–1920 Ford showed no interest in automobile industry parts standardization, since it was already a dominant, vertically integrated firm. More recently Microsoft has become notorious for going its own way with respect to industry standards and America Online has been reluctant to allow access to its instant messaging systems.

However, standards are not always anathema to dominant firms. In some cases, the benefits from standardization can be so compelling that it is worth adopting even from a purely private, profit-maximizing perspective.

Shapiro and Varian (1998a) describe why using a simple equation:

your value = your share × total industry value.

When "total industry value" depends strongly on the size of the market, adopting a standard may increase total value so much that it overcomes the possible dilution in market share.

Besen and Farrell (1994) survey the economic literature on standards formation. They illustrate the strategic issues by focusing on a standards-adoption problem with two firms championing incompatible standards, such as the Sony Betamax and VHS technologies for videotape. Each of these technologies exhibits network effects – indirect network effects in this particular example.

Following Besen and Farrell (1994) we describe the three forms of competition in standards setting.

Standards war Firms compete to determine the standard.

Standards negotiation Both firms want a standard, but disagree about what the standard should be.

Standards leader One firm leads with a proprietary standard, the other firm wants to interoperate with the existing standard.

9.1 Standards wars

With respect to standards wars, Besen and Farrell (1994) identify common tactics such as (1) penetration pricing to build an early lead, (2) building alliances with suppliers of complementary products, (3) expectations management such as bragging about market share or product pre-announcements, and (4) commitments to low prices in the future.

It is not hard to find examples of all of these strategies. Penetration pricing has already been described above. A nice recent example of building alliances is the DVD Forum, which successfully negotiated a standard format in the (primarily Japanese) consumer electronics industry, and worked with the film industry to ensure that sufficient content was available in the appropriate format at low prices.

The DVD player has been a huge and somewhat unlikely success. It managed to compete effectively with a well-entrenched incumbent technology, the VCR, even though the DVD player was a read-only device, unlike the VCR, and hence had no standalone value. Starting the (indirect) network effects was thus particularly difficult. The DVD Forum did an excellent job in pushing for low prices and by defending the DVD standard against the Divx threat (Dranove and Gandal, 2000).

Hollywood also helped negotiate intellectual property licensing deals between Sony and Philips, in part by standing firm on the point that they would not produce content unless there was a common format.

Hollywood had less interest in the standards for writable DVDs – in fact, they might be said to be outright hostile to the idea. Without a "referee," the industry fragmented into three initially incompatible standards. We are now seeing a potential standards battle brewing for the next generation of DVDs, involving Sony and Toshiba. (Dvorak, Wingfield, and McBride, 2004).

Expectations management is very common; when there were two competing standards for 56 Kbit/s modems, each producer advertised that it had an 80 percent market share. In standards wars, there is a very real sense in which the product that people expect to win, *will* win. Nobody wants to be stranded with an incompatible product, so convincing potential adopters that you have the winning standard is critical.

Pre-announcements of forthcoming products are also an attractive ploy, but can be dangerous, since customers may hold off purchasing your current product in order to wait for the new one. This happened, for example, to the Osborne portable computer in the mid-eighties.

Finally, there is the low-price guarantee. When Microsoft introduced Internet Explorer it announced that it was free and would always be free. This was a signal to consumers that they would not be subject to lock-in if they adopted the Microsoft browser. Netscape countered by saying that its products would always be open source. Each competitor played to its strength, but it seems that Microsoft had the stronger hand.

9.2 Standards negotiations

The standards negotiation problem is akin to the classic battle of the sexes game: each player prefers a standard to no standard, but each prefers its own standard to the other's.

As in any bargaining problem, the outcome depends critically on the threat point – the payoff the parties receive if the negotiations break down. The better off a bargainer is if the negotiations fail, the more concessions he will be able to extract from his counterpart. Thus it is common to see companies continuing to develop proprietary solutions, even while engaged in standards negotiation.

Sometimes standards are negotiated under the oversight of official standards bodies, such as the International Telecommunications Union (ITU), the American National Standards Institute (ANSI), the Internet Engineering Task Force (IETF), or any of dozens of other standards-setting bodies. These bodies have the advantage of experience and authority; however, they tend to be rather slow moving. In recent years, there have been many ad hoc standards bodies that have been formed to create a single standard. The standards chosen by these ad hoc groups may not be as good as with the traditional bodies, but they are often developed much more quickly. See Libicki et al. (2000) for a description of standards setting involving the Internet and Web.

Of course, there is often considerable mistrust in standards negotiation, and for good reason. Typically participating firms are required to disclose any technologies for which they own intellectual property that may be relevant to the negotiations. Such technologies may eventually be incorporated into the final standard, but only after reaching agreements that they will be licensed on "fair, reasonable, and non-discriminatory terms." But it is not uncommon to see companies fail to disclose *all* relevant information in such negotiations, leading to accusations of breach of faith or legal suits.

Another commonly used tactic is for firms to cede the control of a standard to an independent third party, such as one of the bodies mentioned above. Microsoft has recently developed a computer language called C# that it hopes will be a competitor to Java. It has submitted the language to ECMA, a computer industry standards body based in Switzerland. Microsoft correctly realized that, in order to convince anyone to code in C#, it would have to relinquish control over the language. However, the extent to which it has actually released control is still unclear. Babcock (2001) reports that there may be blocking patents on aspects of C#, and ECMA does not require prior disclosure of such patents, as long as Microsoft is willing to license them on non-discriminatory terms.

9.3 Standards leader

A typical example is where a large, established firm wants to maintain a proprietary standard, but a small upstart, or a group of small firms, wants to interconnect with that standard. In some cases, the proprietary standard may be protected by intellectual property laws. In other cases, the leader may choose to change its technology frequently to keep the followers behind. Frequent upgrades have the advantage that the leader also makes its own installed base obsolete, helping to address the durable-goods monopoly problem mentioned earlier.

Another tactic for the follower is to use an adapter (Farrell and Saloner, 1992). AM and FM radio never did reach a common standard, but they now peacefully co-exist in a common system. Similarly, "incompatible" software systems can be made to interoperate by building appropriate converters and adapters. Sometimes this is done with the cooperation of the leader, sometimes without.

For example, the open-source community has been very clever in building adapters to Microsoft's standards through reverse engineering. Samba, for example, is a system that runs on Unix machines that allows them to interoperate with Microsoft networks. Similarly, there are many open-source converters for Microsoft applications software such as Word and Excel.

9.4 Cost advantages of standardization

The economic literature on standardization has tended to focus on strategic issues, but there are also considerable cost savings due to economies of scale in manufacture and risk reduction. Thompson (1954) describes the early history of the US automobile industry, emphasizing these factors.

He shows that the smaller firms were interested in standardization in order to reap sufficient economies of scale to compete with Ford and GM, who initially showed no interest in standardization efforts. Small suppliers were also interested in standardization, since that allowed them to diversify the risk associated with supplying idiosyncratic parts to a single assembler.

The Society of Automotive Engineers (SAE) carried out the automotive industry standardization process which yielded many cost advantages to producers. By the late 1920s Ford and GM began to see the advantages of standardization, and joined the effort, focusing at first on the products of complementors (tires, petroleum products, and the like) but eventually playing a significant role in automobile parts standardization.

10 Systems effects

It is common in high-technology industries to see products that are useless unless they are combined into a system with other products: hardware is useless without software, DVD players are useless without content, and operating systems are useless without applications. These are all examples of *complements*, that is, goods whose value depends on their being used together.

Many of the examples we have discussed involve complementarities. Lock-in often occurs because users must invest in complementary products, such as training, to effectively use a good. Direct network effects are simply a symmetric form of complementarities: a fax machine is most useful when there are many other fax machines. Indirect network effects or chicken-and-egg problems are also a form of systems effects. Standards involve a form of complementarity in that they are often designed to allow for seamless interconnection of components (one manufacturer's DVDs will play on another manufacturer's machine).

Systems of complements raise many important economic issues. Who will do the system integration: the manufacturer, the end user, or some intermediary, such as an original equipment manufacturer (OEM)? How will the value be divided up among the suppliers of complementarity? How will bottlenecks be overcome, and how will the system evolve?

This is a vast topic, and I cannot do justice to the whole set of issues. I will limit my discussion to the most-studied issue: the pricing of complements, a topic first studied by Cournot (1838).

In one chapter of this work, Cournot analyzed the strategic interactions between producers of complementary products, considering a market with two companies: a monopoly zinc producer and a monopoly copper producer. These two supplied a large number of other companies that combined the metals to produce brass. Cournot asked what would happen to the price of brass if the copper and zinc producers merged.

Let us assume that one unit of copper and one unit of zinc combine to create one unit of brass. Competition will push the price of brass down to its cost, which will simply be the sum of the two prices. Demand for brass can then be written as $D(p_1 + p_2)$. Given our assumptions about the technology, this is also the demand for copper and zinc.

The copper producer, say, wants to maximize the profit of producing copper:

$$\max_{p_1} p_1 D(p_1 + p_2).$$

Here we have assumed that the cost of copper production is zero for simplicity. The zinc producer has the analogous problem;

$$\max_{p_2} p_2 D(p_1 + p_2).$$

If the two complementary monopolists merged, they would solve the joint profit maximization problem

$$\max_{p_1, p_2} (p_1 + p_2) D(p_1 + p_2).$$

Cournot showed that the complementary monopolists would set prices that were higher than if they merged. The intuition is simple. If the copper producer cuts its price, brass producers will buy more zinc, thereby increasing the profits of the zinc producer. But the zinc producer's additional profits are irrelevant to the copper producer, making it reluctant to cut its price too much. The result is that the copper producer sets a price that is higher than the price that would maximize joint profits.

If, however, the copper and zinc producers merged, the merged entity would take into account that the price of copper affected the demand for zinc and set a lower price for both copper and zinc than independent producers would. Hence, a merger of complementors is a win all the way around: prices fall, making producers *and* consumers better off.

Of course a merger is only one way that prices might be coordinated; there are many other possibilities. Consider again the formula for a complementor's profit:

$$p_1 D(p_1 + p_2).$$

Cutting p_1 may or may not increase profit, depending on elasticity of demand. But cutting p_2 definitely increases revenue for firm 1 in all circumstances. There are a variety of ways a firm might induce a complementor to cut its price.

> *Integrate* One complementor acquires the other, forming a merged entity which internalizes the externality. We have discussed the classic Cournot analysis above.
>
> *Collaborate* The firms set up a formula for revenue sharing, then one firm sets the price of the joint system. For example, an aircraft manufacturer and an engine manufacturer will agree on a revenue-sharing arrangement, then the aircraft manufacturer will negotiate a price for the entire system with customers.
>
> *Negotiate* A firm may commit to cutting its price if the other firm also cuts its price. This apparently went on in the DVD industry, where both the content and players were introduced at relatively low prices, since the participants recognized that a low price for the entire system was critical to ensure its adoption.

Nurture One firm works with others to reduce their costs. For example, Adobe works with printer manufacturers to ensure that they can effectively use its technology.

Commoditize One firm attempts to stimulate competition in the other's market, thereby pushing down prices. Microsoft, for example, has established the Windows Compatibility Lab, to ensure that hardware manufacturers all produce to a common standard. This helps facilitate competition, pushing down the price of hardware.

All of these factors work towards reducing prices, thereby gaining some of the welfare benefits associated with competition. This is especially important since many of the other factors we discussed tend to lead towards high industry concentration ratios and monopoly power. When competitors are not present to discipline monopoly pricing, complementors may sometimes play a similar role.

11　Computer mediated transactions

More and more transactions are being mediated by computers. As we have seen, the data gathered can be mined for information about consumer behavior, allowing for various forms of price discrimination. But this is not the only function that transactions-mediating computers can play. They can also allow firms to contract on aspects of transactions that were previously unobservable.

Consider, for example, the video rental industry. Until 1998, distributors sold pre-recorded videotapes to rental outlets to be hired out for home viewing. The tapes sold for around $60 apiece, far in excess of marginal cost. The rental stores, naturally enough, economized on their purchases, leading to queues for popular movies.

In 1998 the industry came up with a new contractual form: studios provided videotapes to rental stores for a price between zero and $8, and then split revenue for rentals, with the store receiving between 40 and 60 percent of rental revenues. Dana and Spier (2000) and Mortimer (2001) provide further details about these contracts, along with theoretical and empirical analysis of their properties. Mortimer (2001) finds that these contracts increased the revenues of both studios and rental outlets by about 7 percent and consumers benefited substantially. Clearly, the revenue-sharing arrangement offered a superior contractual form over the pre-1998 system.

The interesting thing about this revenue-sharing arrangement is that it was made possible because of computerized record keeping. The cash registers at Blockbuster were intelligent enough to record each rental title and send in an auditable report to the central offices. This allowed all parties in the transaction to verify that revenues were being shared in the agreed-upon way. The fact that the transaction was computer mediated allowed the firms to contract on aspects of the transaction that were previously effectively unobservable, thereby increasing efficiency.

Another example of such computer-enabled contracting occurred in the trucking industry (Hubbard, 2000; Baker and Hubbard, 2000). In the last twenty years, trip recorders and electronic vehicle management systems (EVMS) have become widespread in the industry. Trip recorders are essentially onboard computers that record when the driver turns the engine on or off, how long the truck idles, its average speed, when it accelerates or decelerates, and many other details of operation. EVMS technology does all of this as well, but also collects information about location and transmits information back to the dispatcher in real time. These capabilities help with dispatch coordination, operation efficiency, insurance liability, and fraud detection, making the trucking industry much more cost effective.

As more and more transactions become computer mediated, the costs of monitoring become lower and lower, potentially allowing for more efficient contractual forms.

12 Summary

Better information for incumbents, lock-in, and demand- and supply-side economies of scale suggest that industry structure in high-technology industries will tend to be rather concentrated.

On the other hand, information technology can also reduce minimum efficient scale, thereby relaxing barriers to entry. People value diversity in some areas, such as entertainment, and IT makes it easier to provide such diversity.

Standards are a key policy variable. Under a proprietary standard, an industry may be dominated by a single firm. With an open standard, many firms can interconnect. Consider, for example, the PC industry. The PC itself is a standardized device: there are many motherboard makers, memory chip makers and card providers. There are even several CPU providers, despite the large economies of scale in this industry.

Compare this to the software world, where a single firm dominates the PC operating system and applications environment. What's the difference? The hardware components typically operate according to standardized specifications, so many players can compete in this industry. In the software industry, standards tend to be proprietary. This difference has led to a profound difference in industry structure.

PART TWO

Intellectual property, competition, and information technology

Joseph Farrell and Carl Shapiro

13 Introduction

Professor Varian's overview, "Competition and market power," analyzes a variety of competitive strategies used by high-tech companies. These strategies – such as personalized pricing, lock-in, and the adoption of uniform compatibility standards to fuel bandwagon effects – often rely on intellectual property, typically copyrights or patents. We complement the work of Professor Varian by focusing on this aspect.

First, we give some examples to illustrate how profoundly intellectual property rights influence competitive strategy in the information technology sector.

Like most computer software companies, Microsoft uses copyrights, patents, and secrecy to protect its software programs (notably Windows and Office), worth tens of billions of dollars. Microsoft uses all three of the primary strategies discussed by Professor Varian: price discrimination, lock-in, and exploitation of network effects through the control of proprietary interfaces. Copyright protection strengthens Microsoft's incentives to develop and improve its software, and gives it some control

This contribution was prepared as a companion to the Mattioli Lectures delivered by Hal R. Varian, "Economics of Information Technology." We thank Hal for his comments and suggestions.

over the interfaces between its desktop software and other software, such as middleware and applications software running on Windows, and interfaces with operating system software that runs the powerful server computers linked with desktop machines in complex computer networks.

Copyright protection is also important to the modern music and movie industry. Of course there was an entertainment industry before copyright – rivals are said to have sent stenographers to Shakespeare's opening nights, and even Dickens (as a foreign author) did not get copyright protection in the United States until 1891. But the modern industry sells its products in forms that are often *technologically* very easy to copy. If anyone buying a CD could legally make unlimited digital copies, music studios such as Sony, Warner, Universal, and Bertelsmann could not extract a significant fraction of the true worth of a recording. The same applies to movies.[1] Although such copying is illegal, enforcement is imperfect, so the music labels and the movie studies are gravely concerned about copying in the digital age. Hence they pursue "digital rights management" ("DRM"), building in technological barriers to supplement the legal ones. Controversy has ignited over whether DRM goes too far beyond preventing sheer piracy and prevents other, desirable uses that would otherwise be considered "fair use." We discuss this further in the copyright section below.

Often, desirable uses are mingled with piracy. For instance, the peer-to-peer file sharing system Napster undoubtedly facilitated piracy; yet it also created a cheaper, more flexible distribution system than the costly traditional physical retail distribution of CDs that bundle multiple songs. The music companies asserted their rights under copyright law to shut down Napster. Just as one might have hoped, they did not want to throw out the efficiency benefits of music downloading, and legal music downloads (typically not for free) are now a rapidly expanding business.

---

[1] Limited sharing, as in libraries, might not cause a problem if it proportionately raises the sharing entity's willingness to pay (because it makes a group purchase). Indeed, one could argue that this is the basis of movie theaters: the theater buys a showing right from the studio, and its willingness to pay is based on collecting from the audience. See, for instance, Varian (2000).

Likewise, several movie studies recently formed a joint venture, Movielink, to promote a web site offering legal (again, not for free) movie downloads.

The music labels and movie studios, of course, are just one layer in the entertainment value chain. Two other layers that raise interesting information technology and copyright issues are the retail distributors and the artists themselves. Traditional retail distribution is being challenged in many industries by Internet-based (or even phone-based) ordering with shipping direct to consumers. Information technology makes that process much more efficient, and also enables services such as Netflix's or Amazon's personalized recommendation services. In the case of goods that *are* information, such as music and video entertainment, the shipping component can also become very easy and cheap. Meanwhile, though, information technology also makes traditional retail distribution (especially inventory control) more efficient.

Information technology alters competitive conditions among artists, both horizontally and vertically. Horizontally, information technology may strengthen an increasing-returns "superstar" effect. There are many good tenors, and in the early twentieth century there were hundreds of them who could fill a concert hall on any given evening, even though Enrico Caruso was the superstar of the day. Now, the general public identifies "tenor" with just three performers: José Carreras, Placido Domingo, and Luciano Pavarotti – to such a degree that the Federal Trade Commission charged Vivendi and Warner with restricting competition for audio and video compositions involving "The Three Tenors" in violation of US antitrust laws.[2] Vertically, information technology might work in an opposite direction, enhancing competition and lowering entry barriers by enabling new artists to have their output heard by an international niche audience and perhaps grow from there. In movies, a $500 digital camcorder and a web site can expose a novice movie-maker's work to niche audiences worldwide. Of course, performers have always been able to expose

---

[2] In the Matter of Polygram Holding, Inc.; Decca Music Group Limited; UMG Recordings, Inc.; and Universal Music & Video Distribution Corp., Docket No. 9298, http://www.ftc.gov/os/caselist/d9298.htm.

their work to small audiences – but performing in a café draws a small audience from the neighborhood, while performing on the Internet draws a (perhaps small but potentially unlimited) audience from around the world, so that much more specialization is possible. Many artists certainly hope that the enormous potential of the Internet as a distribution vehicle, combined with its ability to enable stronger and more precisely targeted word-of-mouth recommendations, will erode the power they see being held by the large distribution companies. The hope that information technology will erode the cut taken by intermediaries is shared by authors and other types of artists.

Turning to patents, information technology firms such as IBM, Intel, Hewlett-Packard, and Motorola receive hundreds, if not thousands, of patents each year. They may use their patent portfolios offensively to keep out competitors in certain market niches, defensively to negotiate cross licenses with other firms holding their own patents, or as profit centers by entering into licensing agreements that generate substantial revenues. As the number of patents has grown, and as licensing revenues have multiplied, patents are playing an ever-larger role in competitive strategies in the semiconductor and computer hardware and software industries. The role of patents in these industries appears to be very different from the conventional single-innovation economic literature on patents and patent races, which may more accurately describe pharmaceuticals. While pharmaceuticals are not information technology, they too illustrate how intellectual property supports price discrimination, in that case largely among countries.

Of course, intellectual property rights have long played an important role in industries experiencing rapid technological change. Famous patent disputes arose involving sewing machines, the telegraph, the airplane, and the telephone, to name just a few. And copyright protection has always been important in the publishing industry. But intellectual property rights inherently play a bigger role in establishing competitive advantage in the industries at the heart of the information economy than they did in the agricultural and industrial sectors that used to dominate the economy.

In an agrarian economy, returns accrued to those who owned fertile land, who had the ability to transport agricultural products efficiently to market, and who had sufficient access to capital to withstand unfavorable weather or sharp price fluctuations. Intellectual property, most often in the form of know-how, was important, but such know-how was widely diffused and thus not usually a major source of competitive advantage. Even here, however, intellectual property and similar issues arose. The spice trade was hugely profitable, and producing countries tried to prevent others from obtaining seeds. In modern agriculture, hybrid and engineered seeds (most famously, Monsanto's "Roundup Ready" soybean seeds that are resistant to Monsanto's Roundup pesticide) are protected by intellectual property rights, as are some pesticides, etc.[3]

In the industrial economy, sustainable competitive advantage often revolved around access to low-cost natural resources, control over large manufacturing facilities subject to substantial economies of scale, efficient distribution and marketing, and the ability to manage a large organization with broad geographic reach. While know-how has always been an important source of competitive advantage among manufacturers, and product and process innovations have played a major role in many industries, we would argue that intellectual property rights (especially copyrights) were not as central in the industrial economy as they are in the information economy, where many of the most successful enterprises rely heavily on intellectual property rights to protect their market positions. As a leading example, in the software and information content industries the traditional industrial barriers to entry listed above are lower than in the manufacturing sector and the threat from imitation is more severe.

In what follows, we complement Professor Varian's analysis by showing how intellectual property rights intersect with the competitive strategies he studies. We then build on this observation by exploring how firms are acquiring and asserting intellectual property rights to gain commercial advantage. This leads us naturally into a discussion of whether the existing intellectual property

---

[3] The whole issue of how patent rights involving genetics will be defined and used is terribly important, although outside the scope of this discussion.

regime functions as intended – to stimulate innovation and thus promote long-run competition – or whether the system is out of balance, granting excessive intellectual property rights, and could be improved so as to avoid retarding innovation and/or harming consumers.

In the next section we provide an overview of the basic elements of the intellectual property legal regime in the United States, briefly describing the economic rationales and legal regimes covering copyrights, patents, and trade secrets. We next explain why intellectual property rights underpin each of the competitive strategies studied by Professor Varian. We then move beyond those strategies to look more closely at how the patent system currently is working, or not working, to promote innovation and competition. We close with some observations on possible reform of the patent system.

14 Patents, trade secrets, and copyrights

The intellectual property rights of most interest to economists are copyrights, patents, and trade secrets.[4] Each form of intellectual property has its unique characteristics and role to play.

The United States Constitution provides explicitly for copyrights and patents. The enabling provision (Article I, §8) states that: "Congress shall have Power . . . To Promote the Progress of Science and useful Arts, by securing for Limited Times to Authors and Inventors, the exclusive Right to their Writings and Discoveries."

14.1 Copyrights

We are all familiar with copyrighted works such as books, musical compositions, or movies. Copyright is meant to protect the particular *expression* of an idea. Compared with patents (see below),

---

[4] Trademarks, another form of intellectual property, are most relevant for issues involving brands, reputation, and consumer information. We do not discuss trademarks here.

copyrights are "narrow" in the sense that they do not prevent others from creating or distributing similar works: the copyright on one movie does not prevent others from making movies with similar themes or plot lines. In this sense, copyright law is designed to protect literal copying of creative works – for example publishing an author's book without his or her permission or distributing a musical performance over the Internet without the permission of the company that owns the copyright to that performance. Copyrights may be thought of as granting "mini-monopolies," in the sense that a single book or song has a "monopoly," i.e. represents a unique, differentiated product. Nevertheless, historically, copyrights have not conferred a great deal of market power: there are many substitutes for any given book or piece of music, and when copyrights have threatened to confer such power, their protection is often weakened.[5]

While copyrights are quite "narrow," in the sense just described, they are very long lived. In 1998, the US Congress passed the Copyright Term Extension Act (CTEA), under which most copyrights run until seventy years after the author's death. Previously, under the 1976 Copyright Act, most copyrights lasted until fifty years after the author's death. Congress has repeatedly extended copyrights; back in 1790, copyright protection lasted for only fourteen years, renewable for a second fourteen-year term, after which the work would enter the public domain. Sadly, these extensions have typically included copyrights *already issued*, which is extremely hard to justify on the basis of encouraging or rewarding creative works. After all, once works lose their copyright protection they enter the public domain and are more readily available for others to use and build upon. Evidently, the US Congress has been influenced by pressure from holders of copyrights on valuable works that were nearing expiration. (An example often cited is Disney and the copyright on Mickey Mouse.) Nevertheless, the CTEA was upheld by the US Supreme Court, which ruled that, while perhaps

---

[5] See Menell (2003). Incidentally, the same is true for trademarks. While it is very easy to obtain a trademark – one does not have to establish any innovation to qualify – the resulting trademark may be weakened or even lost if significant market power results. When a brand name such as Kleenex becomes "generic" it is no longer protected.

dubious as a matter of public policy, retroactive copyright extensions were consistent with the Constitution.[6]

Although some have argued that the law has escaped this problem, there is a risk that when copyright law is applied to computer software some of these long-lived copyrights confer far more market power than copyrights on books or music ever did, and far more than is appropriate given the contribution of the copyright holder.[7] This is for two reasons. First, copyrighted computer software, such as Microsoft Windows, can have far greater economic significance than any single book, musical composition, or movie. Second, copyrights can interact with network effects/interfaces and turn what might initially have been rather "arbitrary" choices (with many alternatives) into "essential" choices (with no good alternatives) once users standardize on a product or interface. The greatest power seems to result when the design choices protected by copyright define an *interface* that lets other software be compatible with the copyrighted software in question. If network effects are strong, a copyright including interface protocols can thus confer a good deal of market power.

For example, in the early 1990s the Lotus 1-2-3 spreadsheet software was widely used – indeed, some called its early versions the PC's first "killer app." Borland offered a rival spreadsheet, Quattro Pro, that emulated the Lotus user interface and offered "macro compatibility" so that users could transfer their own programs (macros) written for Lotus 1-2-3 to Quattro Pro. Lotus sued Borland for copyright infringement, and initially won, but the Supreme Court upheld (equally divided and without comment) an appeals court ruling that Lotus's copyright did not enable it to stop Borland from emulating the user interface.[8] Many observers (including one of us) had argued for this result because the user interface, even if considered initially arbitrary "expression," acquired *ex post* market power as users saved important

---

[6] *Eldred* vs. *Ashcroft*, US Supreme Court, decided 15 January 2003; available at http://www.supremecourtus.gov/opinions/02pdf/01-618.pdf.

[7] See Menell (2003), both for the argument that copyright law has sorted this out and for some of the mis-steps along the way.

[8] The lower court decision is 49 F. 3d 807 (1st Circuit, 1995); the (uninformative) Supreme Court ruling is at 516 US 233 (1996).

spreadsheets, learned to use the product, and crafted macros.[9] Both in the US and in Europe, there are now fairly extensive rights to reverse engineer and copy software so as to achieve compatibility, both for complements and for substitutes.[10] Even the Digital Millennium Copyright Act (DMCA) (section 1201(f)) recognizes this right.

To cite another important example, Microsoft's copyrights on Microsoft Windows and on Microsoft Office cannot prevent others from making operating systems or productivity suites with similar features or functionality, but they can, especially combined with secrecy, prevent others from copying some of the file formats or other interfaces associated with these widely used programs. Indeed, Microsoft places great value on its ability to protect the interface between its Windows operating system running on desktop computers and operating systems running on servers. Microsoft fought vigorously in its antitrust case with the US government to limit any duties imposed on it to open up or license the Windows program interfaces.[11]

As these examples illustrate, the scope of copyright protection can have very significant implications for competition and innovation. More examples can be found in the debate surrounding the proper copyright treatment afforded to databases since the Supreme Court's 1991 *Feist* decision, holding that some creativity must go into the creation of a database for it to qualify for copyright protection.[12]

---

[9] See "Amicus Brief of Economics Professors and Scholars in Support of Respondent," available at http://elsa.berkeley.edu/users/woroch/amicus.txt. To economists, an odd feature of the case was that *Borland* argued that *Lotus* had put considerable research and effort into the design of its user interface. While this would if anything have helped Lotus had it been a patent case, in a copyright case this helped Borland argue that there were no comparably efficient alternative interfaces, so that if Lotus got copyright protection on the interface, that would give it market power in a way that copyright is not meant to do.

[10] See for instance Samuelson and Scotchmer (2002).

[11] Unhappiness with Microsoft's licensing program regarding interfaces between the desktop and servers erupted in early 2004 as the Department of Justice told the Court overseeing its settlement with Microsoft that it was not satisfied with Microsoft's performance in this area.

[12] See *Feist Publications* vs. *Rural Telephone Service Co.*, 499 US 340. In *Feist*, a simple list of names and addresses did not merit copyright protection. See http://www.copyright.gov/reports/dbase.html for a summary of the issues in this area as of 1997.

We are currently witnessing a very active debate over the role of copyright, and whether copyright law must change, in the digital age. On the one hand, certain rights holders express grave concern that modern information technology is permitting piracy to become rampant, and that the Internet is serving as "one giant copying machine" that steals creative material from authors, composers, and artists. These people seek to mandate technologies that would prevent or limit unauthorized reproduction of copyrighted works. They also seek broad powers to identify individuals engaged in copyright infringement, and stiff penalties for those found to have used copyrighted materials without permission. At the same time, many other observers express concerns that copyright law is serving us poorly in the information age as rights holders use technology to prevent innocent or socially desirable uses of their works that would otherwise be perfectly legal. These critics assert that copyrights now confer too much power, either to control how works are used or to keep works out of the public domain for many years, and that "fair use" is being defined too narrowly.[13] Napster not only threatened music studios' intellectual property: it was also innovative in its own right.

Both sides in this debate predict a decline in creative activity. But one side predicts that this decline will result as widespread piracy undermines the incentives to create, while the other side predicts that the decline of creativity will result from sharp limits on the public's ability to use copyrighted works and a greatly reduced public domain. These points of view need not be empirical *alternatives*: it could well be that information technology does indeed encourage piracy and that this is inefficient, *and* that digital rights management allows and encourages copyright holders to limit the use of digital works in ways that stifle complementary creativity and go far beyond limiting piracy (even though the holder of a clear property right does not usually want to limit complementary innovation *as such*). A key question would then be whether some more "refined" public policies than (for instance) the widely criticized DMCA could stem piracy without forcing

---

[13] For a recent and entertaining summary of this growing criticism of the copyright system, see Boynton (2004). See also Mann (1998).

or encouraging copyright holders to impose other, socially (and possibly privately) undesirable, restrictions. This debate has generated a great deal of heat, and rather less light. At its worst, media companies complain of rampant and irresponsible piracy while seeking retroactive copyright extensions, and digital freedom fighters claim that "information wants to be free" and rail against corporate greed. As economists, we hope we can take the debate in a more constructive direction by identifying more carefully crafted policies that control piracy without curtailing fair use or greatly shrinking the public domain. But we must recognize that the two polar viewpoints do conflict at the policy level, if there are no such policies. They also represent a fundamental clash of views about the sources of innovation and creativity.

The *incentives school* focuses on whether an innovator can capture a large portion of the benefit of his or her creation. Implicitly, this school thinks of innovation that is "one percent inspiration, ninety-nine percent perspiration" (to quote Edison). Perspiration will be more forthcoming if it is well paid. Moreover, it may not much matter whether a hundred people (or firms) have strong incentives, or whether just one does: if anyone has a strong enough incentive to sweat, he or she will do so. On this view, innovative efforts, like many other investments, are driven primarily by the return they can generate, after adjusting for risk. It seems fair to say that this school of thought presently has the ascendancy in policy circles.

The *openness school*, by contrast, thinks that it somewhat misses the point to focus on a few firms' incentives for working harder. First of all, there are incentives – often quite strong – for innovation and creativity quite aside from intellectual property. At the level of firms, innovation can help build reputation, and achieve time-to-market advantages: indeed, a widely cited survey of corporations found that intellectual property is seldom firms' primary means of achieving rewards for innovation.[14] At the level of individuals, invention – which can be fun and/or easy once inspiration strikes – can be rewarding in career advancement, social

---

[14] See Levin et al. (1987). More recently, see Cohen, Nelson, and Walsh (2000).

recognition, or self-esteem. And, the openness school argues, it is important that many independent minds work on any given problem, because the next creative idea could come from anywhere. This school of thought is represented by such advocates as Lawrence Lessig (2001), who argues powerfully for an "innovation commons" in his book, *The Future of Ideas*, and who helped found the "Creative Commons" (http://creativecommons.org/) to promote this concept through innovative licensing schemes. The openness school stresses the role of the public domain and fair use in spurring creativity.[15]

Surely this clash is an empirical matter: presumably some kinds of innovation, in some industries, demand strong incentives, and perspiration may be straightforward, if uncomfortable. For those cases, which might include, for instance, modern pharmaceutical development, the incentives school probably has the stronger position. Other kinds of innovation, perhaps in other industries, are fun and creative, or the by-product of other activities attractive in their own right, and – once inspiration strikes – do not demand strong financial incentives. Perhaps there are many industries where current copyright protection goes too far, in that greater openness and weaker protection would do far more to increase the supply of creative works (by expanding the public domain

---

[15] As economists, we see "fair use" as limiting the package of rights that are granted to a copyright holder. Following the Coase Theorem (Coase, 1937), one can ask whether the assignment of such rights matters, and whether private parties should be permitted to enter into contracts that restrict or expand the rights of those using the copyrighted materials. The initial assignment of rights affects the return to creating copyrighted works and thus has efficiency consequences. One may also view fair-use doctrine as similar to the law on interpretation of private contracts: by assigning rights that "most" parties will want to agree to anyhow, the law can save on negotiation and transaction costs, including costs due to strategic manipulation such as hold-up. In this interpretation, fair use should be the best estimate of the court, or the legislature, of what most copyright holders and buyers/licensees would have agreed on had they bothered to negotiate the relevant terms. But this perspective omits the interests of third parties, as do some explicit terms in copyright licenses. For example, consider a software product whose "shrink-wrap agreement" forbids licensees to publish reviews, or at least negative reviews, of the product. (We are told that Autonomy Systems, which describes itself as "the leading provider of software infrastructure that automates operations on unstructured information," www.autonony.com, uses such provisions in some of its software licenses.) Because third parties are affected, i.e. because of informational externalities, one can argue that certain rights of copyright licensees should be inalienable. We do not explore this area further here.

and the scope of fair use) than it would do to reduce the supply of creative works through a direct incentive effect.

We can illustrate the theoretical ambiguity with a modest sketch of a model. Suppose that a single firm's probability of developing an innovation is $p(x)$ if its reward for success would be x. Presumably the function p is increasing, but it might be either concave or (in some range) convex. Concavity would indicate that there are diminishing returns in the probability of success by a single firm as a function of the prize from successful development. Convexity would correspond to increasing returns. But the shape of p is not the end of the story, because it is socially valuable to have at least one firm develop the innovation, but the gains from a second, third, or ninth discovery of the same innovation are far smaller, perhaps zero.[16] For simplicity let us assume that duplicative discovery is valueless, so that policy should aim to maximize the probability that *at least one* firm develops the innovation, which we denote by T. If different firms' discoveries are statistically independent, then this probability is given by:

$$T = 1 - \prod_i (1 - p(x_i)).$$

Now consider the broad sweep of "incentives" versus "openness" policies. We might interpret "incentives" policies as aiming to maximize the maximum among firms' incentives: it is important for someone to have a strong incentive to work hard, but since invention need only happen once, it need only be one firm. On the other hand, we might interpret "openness" policies as aiming to maximize the number of firms who have a prospect – perhaps loosely interpreted as some minimal threshold of incentive – for innovating. While it does not necessarily correspond to any specific policy choice, we can try to sketch the tradeoffs by thinking of total incentives – the sum of all firms' values of x – as constrained to be no more than some sum, X.[17]

---

[16] In reality, duplicative discovery may sharpen product-market competition relative to single-firm discovery, and if different firms discover different "versions" of the innovation there may be further benefits. Still, it seems likely that the incremental benefits decline sharply with the number of independent discoverers.

[17] Notice that in an ideally functioning system, everyone would have x equal to the full social contribution of their innovation (relative, of course, to the but-for

Thus we formalize the policy problem as choosing the values x_i for firms $i = 1, 2, \ldots N$, subject to the constraint that the x_i add up to no more than X, so as to maximize T. This is equivalent to minimizing the logarithm of $(1 - T)$, which is the sum of $\log(1 - p(x_i))$. Therefore if $\log(1 - p(x))$ is convex in x, it pays to focus the incentive and give some firm as strong an incentive as possible (that is $x_i = X$ for one i and $x_j = 0$ for the rest). If $\log(1 - p(x))$ is concave in x, it pays to spread the incentive and set $x_i = X/N$ for all i.[18]

The incentives school has shown how digital technology can be used to engage in widespread copyright infringement. On both equity and efficiency grounds, such piracy should not be ignored. And no economist could deny that reducing the financial return to producing creative works will, *ceteris paribus*, tend to reduce the supply of creative works. By the same token, however, the openness school has done a good job of illustrating the profound long-run social benefits of fair use and the public domain. In all areas, one person's creativity necessarily is influenced by, and builds upon, prior creations. In principle, empirical evidence could show which of these forces is more significant, in which settings, and could thus inform the proper limits of copyright protection in the digital age. Unfortunately, this type of empirical work is unlikely to yield definitive answers, so we expect this debate to remain spirited.

Intriguingly, these competing views are battling not only in the public policy arena, as copyright law is interpreted and redefined in the face of emerging digital technologies, but in the commercial arena as well, especially in the computer software industry. The most visible example of this is the current struggle between Microsoft, promoting its ubiquitous and proprietary Windows operating system, and Linux, the open-source software operating system widely used on server computers. As fascinating as

---

world, which might involve someone else innovating). Thus the total of all values of x might be very large. We are assuming here, to the contrary, that giving one party more incentive comes at the cost of reducing opportunities or incentives for others. We also are not tracking the costs associated with the innovative efforts of the individuals or companies who may make this discovery.

[18] See Bagnoli and Bergstrom (1989) for more applications and theory of log concavity.

we find this particular battle,[19] it should not be seen as a test of one grand view against the other. At best, it is a test of which model (proprietary software vs. open-source software) works better in a particular market niche (operating system software), with its own peculiar fact patterns (such as the substantial advantage enjoyed by Microsoft based on its installed base of Windows desktop machines).[20]

14.2 Patents

14.2.1 PATENT INSTITUTIONS

Inventors who make new, useful, and non-obvious discoveries may apply for patents that give them the legal right to prevent others from practicing their inventions during the lifetime of the patent, typically twenty years. In the US, patents are granted by the Patent and Trademark Office (PTO), although their validity and scope is tested in the Federal courts.[21] Some twenty years ago, Congress established a specialized appeals court to deal with patents, the Federal Circuit Court of Appeals (CAFC).

The patent system very explicitly offers inventors a prize, in the form of exclusive rights. For significant patents, those rights confer monopoly power, and thus impose costs on consumers, most directly in the form of the higher prices resulting from that monopoly power. Society also pays a price associated with this monopoly power relative to the alternative in which the invention is freely made available. One type of social cost arises

---

[19] For a more extended discussion of the adoption of Linux and the associated intellectual property issues, see Varian and Shapiro (2003).

[20] It may also be an imperfect test if assertions of intellectual property (such as recently made by SCO Group, Inc. against Linux) creep into the open-source world. Legally, open-source software is not devoid of intellectual property. Rather, intellectual property is asserted and a licensing agreement promises full and perpetual absence of exclusion or demands for money. This may in part guard against later assertions of intellectual property rights against open-source software. For more on the General Public License used by Linux, see Varian and Shapiro (2003).

[21] We focus here on patent institutions in the United States. However, inventors often file for patents in many countries. We do not address the issue of international harmonization of patent laws.

due to the standard inefficiency or deadweight losses associated with monopoly pricing. Other social costs result from the frictions that arise when patent holders negotiate licenses with possible complementary innovators. Because these costs are substantial, the policy of granting patents only makes economic sense (and should only be applied) in cases where it is sufficiently likely that innovation would be substantially reduced or delayed in the absence of a patent prize to reward successful innovation.[22] This insight is reflected in the legal requirements that the invention be "novel" and "non-obvious." In exchange for the temporary exclusivity associated with the patent grant, the inventor must publicly disclose the workings of the invention.

14.2.2 GROWING NUMBER OF PATENTS

As noted above, many high-tech manufacturers such as IBM, Intel, and Motorola are granted hundreds if not thousands of patents each year. In some respects, this pattern is not new – industrial leaders have long relied on patents as one means of appropriating returns on their R&D and gaining competitive advantage, although research suggests that it has never been the only or even the predominant means of doing so. But the ways in which patents are used has changed markedly over the past twenty years.[23]

Several robust findings emerge from this literature. First, there clearly has been a rapid increase in the overall number of patents issued, especially in the information technology sector, including in particular software patents and business method patents. Second, the propensity to patent, as measured by the number of patents relative to expenditure on R&D, has risen as well. In principle, these patterns could result from a surge in innovation flowing

---

[22] Other systems are, of course, possible, such as government funding of research and development, monetary prizes for successful invention, and the academic compensation models. But these systems seem, at best, useful in limited areas: government funding is critical for basic research, and monetary prizes seem to make sense for those who solve specific, known problems (such as proving Fermat's last theorem, decoding the human genome, or sending a human to Mars). For better or worse, we are stuck with the patent system as the primary explicit method by which most inventors receive financial rewards.

[23] For a recent overview, see Gallini (2002).

from a wealth of innovative opportunities. Perhaps the impressive recent advances in basic science and technology have led to greater opportunities for patented invention than in the past.

But there are good reasons to believe that other forces are at work as well.[24] First, creation of the Federal Circuit Court of Appeals appears to have given more power to patent holders. Second, there also appears to have been a shift in the strategic use of patents, with more firms using their patents offensively to exclude rivals and/or collect royalties, thus inducing more firms to seek patents defensively to fend off such tactics. Third, there are widespread reports that the PTO has issued a large number of "questionable" patents, especially in the information technology sector, exacerbating these problems. We discuss reform of the patent system below.

14.2.3 DOES THE PATENT SYSTEM PROVIDE SUITABLE INCENTIVES TO INNOVATE?

Even when it is functioning well, does the patent system provide appropriate incentives for private firms to engage in innovative activities?

Ever since patents were first issued, debate has raged over whether the patent system was working effectively to stimulate innovation: do the property rights associated with patents provide a strong enough incentive for innovation to warrant the costs associated with the resulting monopoly power? This debate continues in full force as patents have become especially important in the information technology sector of the economy. More specifically, since the patent system provides a prize to inventors, in the form of exclusive rights, one might well ask whether that prize is too big, too small, or just sufficient to provide suitable incentives to inventors. Unfortunately, there is no easy or general answer to this question, despite a mountain of theoretical and empirical work devoted to the topic.

A simple, static model can help to illustrate some of the trade-offs involved. Criticism of that same model can show why the

---

[24] See Kortum and Lerner (1998).

underlying question about the magnitude of rewards to patent holders is so tricky to resolve, either theoretically or empirically.

Consider an invention that enables the production of a new product (or service). Assume (for now) that the patent holder sets a single price for its product. Denote the demand for this new product by $P = D(X)$, where P is the price per unit and X is the quantity demanded. The revenues are thus given by $R(X) = XD(X)$. The total gross benefits to consumers if X units are produced are given by $B(X) = \int_0^x D(z)dz$. Consumer surplus is given by $S(X) = B(X) - R(X)$.

Let the cost to the inventor of producing the new product (once the discovery is made) be given by $C(X)$. Then the (post-discovery) profits to the patent holder are given by $\pi(X) = R(X) - C(X)$ if a quantity X is produced. Total post-discovery welfare (profits plus consumer surplus) is given by $W(X) = \pi(X) + S(X) = B(X) - C(X)$.

As usual, the profit-maximizing quantity equates marginal revenue and marginal cost. Call the optimal quantity X^*, with corresponding price $P^* = D(X^*)$, profits $\pi^* = \pi(X^*)$, and consumer surplus $S^* = S(X^*)$. Recall that consumers enjoy surplus even when buying from a monopolist, so long as the monopolist cannot engage in perfect price discrimination. Some consumers value the product above the monopoly price, P^*, and thus enjoy surplus. The magnitude of consumer surplus depends upon the shape of the demand curve. Consumer surplus is large if there are a good number of consumers who place very high value on the new product, but still enough consumers with lower willingness-to-pay so that the profit-maximizing price is modest. Our main point, for now, is that considerable consumer surplus can stem from new products, even those (such as patented pharmaceutical drugs) supplied by a monopolist.[25]

Now we are ready to consider the incentives facing the would-be innovator. Begin with the simple case in which (a) there is only a single firm that recognizes the potential for this particular innovation, and (b) demand for this product comes only at the

---

[25] Consumer surplus may be reduced if the patent holder can engage in price discrimination. In the extreme case of perfect price discrimination, there is no consumer surplus during the lifetime of the patent.

expense of other products that are competitively supplied, and not at the expense of other products supplied by firms with market power.

Suppose that the potential innovator can devote more resources to research in this area and thus increase the probability of successful invention. (The analysis is similar if greater R&D efforts lead to *earlier* invention.) Suppose that the probability of successful invention is $Q = F(Y)$ if the firm spends Y on R&D, where research expenditures have positive but decreasing return, so $F'(Y) > 0$ and $F''(Y) < 0$ for all $Y > 0$. Assuming, for simplicity, that the firm is risk neutral, and thus maximizes expected profits, the firm picks Y to maximize $F(Y)\pi^* - Y$. The firm's optimal level of R&D expenditures, Y^*, is given implicitly by $F'(Y^*) = 1/\pi^*$. The larger are the resulting profits, π^*, the smaller is $1/\pi^*$, and hence $F'(Y^*)$, which requires a larger value of Y^*, since $F''(Y) < 0$. These calculations confirm the intuitive point that the firm will invest more in R&D, the larger are the profits associated with making the invention and obtaining the patent.

In this simple case, the socially optimal level of R&D investment given the patent system, Y^{**}, is larger than the profit-maximizing level of investment, Y^*. The socially optimal level of R&D investment maximizes the expected social returns, $W(Y) = F(Y)(\pi^* + S^*) - Y$. The first-order condition for Y^{**} is given by $F'(Y^{**}) = 1/(\pi^* + S^*)$, which is less than $1/\pi^*$, which equals $F'(Y^*)$. Therefore, we have $F'(Y^{**}) < F'(Y^*)$, which, using $F''(Y) < 0$, implies that $Y^{**} > Y^*$. Intuitively, the profit-maximizing firm does not account for the consumer surplus generated by its invention, S^*, when picking its R&D investment level. Effectively, invention generates a positive externality on consumers.

Therefore, this very simple static model suggests that the patent system provides *insufficient* incentives for inventors. This observation is strengthened once one recognizes that the patent lasts for only twenty years, so the consumer surplus resulting from the invention includes not only the consumer surplus during the first twenty years associated with the monopoly price, but a presumably higher level of consumer surplus associated with competitive prices indefinitely once the patent expires (holding aside issues of whether the patent becomes more or less commercially important

68   JOSEPH FARRELL AND CARL SHAPIRO

over time). When one remembers that the patent holder also must disclose its invention, and other inventions may well build on this patented discovery, the benefits enjoyed by society that are not captured by the patent holder appear to be significant.

While all of these effects are real, the static model presented is too simple to form the basis for such a broad policy conclusion, for at least two important reasons that we now explain.

First and foremost, the model simply assumed that the invention at issue would never have been discovered if not for this particular inventor. This presumption was built in when we assumed in defining $W(Y)$ that the "but-for" world without this firm's invention would be no invention. A very different result would obtain if we assume, instead, that the same invention would have been made a short time later. For example, in March 1876 Alexander Graham Bell received the patent on the telephone, having filed his application two weeks earlier on the same day as Elisha Gray, an employee of Western Union, filed a patent caveat.[26] Such near-simultaneous invention is actually quite common, especially when advances in basic science open up new commercial opportunities that are recognized by many firms who then race to be the first to turn the basic discovery into a practical and useful invention suitable for patent protection. To study this properly requires a dynamic model. Roughly speaking, however, in the static model already presented, $W(Y)$ would be far, far smaller. If we think of measuring all the variables in the static model as present discounted values, $W(Y)$ would correspond to the flow of social benefits for the period of time until someone else made the same discovery. However, the social cost of awarding the patent, the deadweight loss from the patent monopoly, runs for the full twenty years in the patent lifetime.

Therefore, the rewards to the patent holder can easily far exceed his or her social contribution, if indeed the same discovery would likely have been made by another in the near future. This tendency is all the greater if each company invests in R&D not simply to maximize its own return considered in isolation (as assumed above) but in order to accelerate its discovery and thus win the patent

---

[26] See, e.g., Brock (1981), p. 89.

race.[27] In practice, it is usually extremely hard for any agency in charge of issuing patents to tell whether a given invention was a "flash of genius" that no one but the applicant would have come up with any time soon, or "in the air" and likely to have been discovered in the near future by someone else. But at the least we should be wary of patents issued in industries with a very large number of incremental innovations driven by underlying advances in basic science and underlying, widely known technology.

Second, we should account for the fact that patented products are often substitutes for other products that are priced well above marginal cost. Under well-known principles of "profit stealing" there can be excessive incentives for private, profit-maximizing firms to engage in commercial activities that shift business from one firm with market power to another.[28] This is due to the negative externality imposed on the firm losing the customers.[29] Once such "profit stealing" is recognized, it no longer follows that the social returns to invention exceed the private returns, even for an invention that is unlikely to have been discovered any time soon by others. Not surprisingly, there is a large literature on the economics of the patent system.

14.2.4 LICENSING AND THE DIFFUSION OF INNOVATIONS

While the patent confers upon the patent holder the exclusive right to practice his or her invention, patent holders frequently issue licenses permitting others to practice their inventions. Licensing is common in some industries, including much of the information technology sector, but far less common in others, such as pharmaceuticals.

Licensing is important for at least two reasons. First, some patent holders can earn far greater profits by licensing their

---

[27] For an overview of the literature on patent races, see Reinganum (1989).

[28] See for instance Mankiw and Whinston (1986).

[29] Some readers may wonder why "externalities" play a role here, and above when we said that a new product generates positive externalities for consumers, given that there are no "missing markets" in these models. The reason is that pecuniary externalities can give rise to real welfare effects in the presence of market power.

patents than by keeping their inventions to themselves. This is especially clear for a patent holder who has limited presence in the market yet has obtained a patent for technology that is valuable for many large or incumbent suppliers. Second, licensing promotes the usage and diffusion of new technologies. Happily, unlike stronger patent protection, which at best can promote innovation at the expense of diffusion and short-term monopoly power, licensing can simultaneously promote both innovation and diffusion.

Of course, the terms and conditions on which licenses are granted will greatly affect the economic impact of licensing. Under a simple license, the patent holder grants the licensee the right to use the patented invention and in return the licensee pays license fees, usually either an agreed fixed fee or a percentage of the revenues earned on products that embody the patented inventions, or both. One or more patents may be licensed in the same transaction. Firms frequently offer package licenses, under which the royalties associated with a group of patents are less than the sum of the royalties offered for the individual constituent patents.

Increasingly, firms are entering into cross licenses. Under a cross license, in exchange for the right to practice A's patented invention, firm B grants firm A the right to practice firm B's own patented invention. Effectively, cross licenses are a form of barter using patents. Cross licenses without running royalties are especially attractive and efficient from an *ex post* competitive perspective: they permit the diffusion and use of patented technology without elevating the marginal costs of either party. Monetary payments, either one-way or two-way, may also be included in cross licenses. The use and prevalence of cross licensing varies greatly across industries.

In the semiconductor industry, many of the larger firms enter into cross licenses involving a number of patents, or entire patent portfolios. These broad cross-licensing agreements can cover existing patents, current patent applications, and even future patents for which applications have not yet been filed. When two large semiconductor firms enter into a broad, forward-looking cross license, they have effectively chosen to replace the patent thicket that would otherwise result from the operation of the patent system with a largely "patent-free zone," at least vis-à-vis each other.[30] Perhaps this judgment suggests that the "default" patent regime has become dysfunctional in the semiconductor industry. Manufacturers in that industry seem to despise those firms who accumulate (or acquire) intellectual property without themselves being producers: a manufacturer cannot use its own patents "defensively" against such firms. Naturally, this raises the question of whether non-producing firms that obtain patents are being rewarded in ways that are excessive given their actual contributions. If such a firm obtains a patent for a valid innovation that would not have taken place without that firm's innovative effort, the mere fact that a non-producing firm lacks interest in cross licensing is no reason why that firm should not be able to assert its patent rights. However, one might view the widespread dissatisfaction with such non-producing firms as signaling that (in the industry view) many of the patents issued are "bad," but that, as long as all patent-holders are also producers, the industry has a decent workaround.

14.3 Trade secrets

Trade secrets are useful information that individuals or companies possess and do not share widely with others. Trade secrets are a form of intellectual property and receive legal protections, most importantly to prevent *theft* of trade secrets. There is no fixed lifetime to the protection afforded to trade secrets.

However, unlike copyright and patents, trade secrets lose protection once they leak out into the public domain through reverse engineering or disclosure by the owner of the secret. Therefore, owners must be vigilant about protecting their trade secrets and

---

[30] One concern is that incumbents with large patent portfolios can thus declare a type of "patent truce" while still keeping out would-be entrants who lack a sufficient portfolio to join the "club." We consider this line of reasoning interesting but incomplete.

preventing their unauthorized use. Lawsuits involving alleged theft of trade secrets are common when employees privy to them go to work for rival firms. Trade secrets can be licensed; of course, such licenses must contain provisions to make sure that the licensee does not transmit the secret to third parties without the permission of its owner.

Trade secret protection is weak in that the owner of a trade secret cannot prevent others from using the same know-how if they discover it independently. Therefore, a company which develops new technology often faces a complex decision whether to keep the new technology secret or file for a patent. If the company opts for the trade secret route and prevents the know-how from entering the public domain, the law will help it prevent others from stealing its secrets. However, the secret might be rediscovered independently and either enter the public domain (for all to use) or, worse, be patented by the later discoverer, in which case the original innovator could even be forced either to stop using the technology it originally discovered or to purchase a license from the patent holder.[31] Alternatively, the original discoverer can file for a patent on its new technology, and if it gets one, will get the right to prevent others from using it. Of course, the *quid pro quo* for obtaining a patent is the disclosure of the invention to the public, making it more likely that other firms will attempt to use the patented invention, perhaps invent around it, and even build on it to obtain their own patents. Additionally, in some cases, the patent may be hard to enforce. For example, for a patent involving process technology, the patent holder may find it very difficult to determine which other firms are in fact using its patented processes. Furthermore, the patent will last for only twenty years, while trade secrets can be kept indefinitely.

Having discussed intellectual property protection in general, and identified some broad issues, we now consider how information technology supports the three general strategies of differentiation, lock-in and proprietary standards.

[31] The original inventor cannot prevent another from patenting the discovery by arguing that its usage constituted "prior art," since discoveries that are concealed do not qualify as "prior art" under patent law.

15 Differentiation of products and prices

Professor Varian illustrates how firms use information technology to engage in price discrimination. As he notes, price discrimination may be an especially attractive tactic in information markets, because the high fixed ("first-copy") costs and low marginal costs for information goods imply that entry will not normally take place to the point where competition forces firms to price near marginal cost to all customers. As usual, price discrimination requires some degree of market power, typically based on offering a differentiated product, and the ability to prevent arbitrage. For the software and content industries, copyright protection is critical to product differentiation (by preventing unauthorized copying) and often important as well for the prevention of arbitrage (through restrictions on sublicensing or transfer of the license, included in the original licensing of the copyrighted material, that prevent "resale").

An interesting illustration is how the music industry has responded to online distribution via the Internet. One might hope that the industry would welcome and take advantage of a new, low-cost distribution medium. If piracy can be controlled, either through legal means or technological means including "digital rights management," online music distribution should be a boon both to artists and to the music labels that sign up and promote them and distribute their music (though not for traditional music retailers unless they can somehow transfer their brand names or other assets to online distribution). Distribution costs could fall dramatically. After all, several dollars of the $15 retail price for a typical music CD goes to the retailer. If a music label could save this distribution cost, and the cost of producing physical disks, it could either lower its prices by several dollars per CD or enjoy a bigger profit margin (or a combination).

The music industry is now pursuing online distribution. Sony and Universal initially formed a joint venture called Pressplay, while Warner, EMI, and Bertelsmann promoted an alternative service known as MusicNet. Users complained that these early services imposed so many restrictions on the use of the downloaded music that they were not very attractive (for example MusicNet initially allowed only streaming or time-limited downloads), but since then legal music download services, most notably Apple's iTunes, have become more user friendly and increasingly popular. But this embracing of online distribution has been slow; the industry first saw it as a threat, much as the movie industry initially viewed the VCR. While a low-cost complement to the industry will have long-term benefits, in the short run it has threatened to disrupt existing pricing models and, worse, to facilitate piracy. The peer-to-peer file-sharing network Napster became a familiar name, although the vast majority of sharing on Napster involved piracy. Eventually, the music companies were able to shut down Napster because of copyright infringement.[32] Whether less centralized file-sharing networks such as Grokster can survive the legal attack of the music industry remains to be seen.[33]

Online music illustrates the differentiation, or versioning, of products and prices. Firms can and do offer a variety of terms and conditions under which a piece of music can be used: Does the customer purchase the right to play it once, or multiple times, or for a limited period? Can the customer transfer the music to a mobile device or burn it to a CD? Are customers permitted to make multiple copies for use on different devices? Clearly, the licensed rights associated with even a single tune can be sliced and diced in a multitude of ways. More broadly, music can be sold as concerts (from which ancillary or complementary revenues such as parking and sales of promotional items may be very important), and/or as recordings, with complex possibilities of substitution and complementarity (you may be more rather than less likely to buy a CD after attending a concert, or if a friend of yours did so).

---

[32] See *A&M Records Inc.* vs. *Napster Inc.*, 239 F.3d 1004 (Ninth Circuit, 2001). Interestingly, Roxio purchased Pressplay in May 2003 and re-launched this service under the Napster name.

[33] As of this writing, the Ninth Circuit is considering the Grokster case, *Metro-Goldwyn-Mayer Studios, Inc., et. al.* vs. *Grokster Ltd.* Central to this case is the interpretation of the Supreme Court's opinion in the landmark "Sony Betamax" case, *Sony Corporation of America* vs. *Universal City Studios, Inc.*, 464 US 417 (1984), which protected technologies with substantial non-infringing uses from secondary liability from copyright infringement, even if those technologies were also used in ways that infringed on copyrights. For an analysis of the Grokster case, see, for example, the Brief Amici Curiae of 40 Intellectual Property and Technology Law Professors Supporting Affirmance, available at http://www.sims.berkeley.edu/~pam/papers.html.

Much the same is true of the movie industry. Originally movies were distributed to theaters and audiences paid the theater for a viewing. Later, studios realized they could sell rights to televise their movies (and the broadcasters could collect money through advertising). VCRs were originally seen as threatening this model, by enabling consumers to watch the movie-with-ads later (time-shifting) and possibly skipping over (or being more willing to leave the room during) the advertisements. Universal Studios sued Sony (the producer of the Betamax VCR) for facilitating consumers' copyright infringement, but the Supreme Court held (see the citation given above) that since Betamax had substantial legitimate uses, Sony was not liable. Although this may have left Betamax *users* liable in principle for copyright infringement, the industry had little chance of preventing home recording and eventually figured out a way to embrace rather than fight the technology. Now, both movie studios and TV networks sell – and rent – tapes and DVDs of their programming. With the advent of digital cable, pay-per-view, whereby customers pay for a single viewing of a movie or other programming, is becoming more and more popular. As broadband connections become more widespread and computers become yet more powerful, we expect this model to spread to movies delivered over the Internet on an on-demand basis rather than via the traditional cable television technical and business model.[34]

Price discrimination is attractive to the music companies for another reason, which has to do with the strength of their copyright protection: the elasticity of demand for online music is likely to be higher than the elasticity of demand for CDs or other forms of music, because of the threat of illegal downloads. After all, the main alternative to *legally* downloading a song for many people may be to download the same song *illegally*. Thus, for many customers, especially those who use computers heavily and have fast online connections, illegally downloaded copies are a close substitute for legal copies.

---

[34] In the US, most residential broadband Internet access is via cable modems, and it is an open question how far cable companies will try to exert control over this trend as it threatens their traditional business model but opens up new possibilities.

The music industry has tried to make illegal downloads a less attractive substitute by public-relations attempts to make people feel guilty about stealing copyrighted music and by suing individuals who illegally make available or download large numbers of music files. The industry has hesitantly begun to authorize legal downloads through Apple's iTunes service (http://www.apple.com/itunes) and others, which offer large libraries of songs, typically at 99 cents each. Unlike earlier legal services, iTunes does not impose stringent restrictions on the use of downloaded material.

Online distribution is less advanced in the movie industry, but the same dynamic is likely to play out over time. Downloading huge movie files will become more practical as broadband Internet access becomes more widespread, as users acquire larger and larger hard drives on which to store them, and as home computers are networked with (or even become) televisions and other home entertainment equipment. Some of the major movie studios (MGM, Paramount, Sony, Universal and Warner), keen not to let an illegal service similar to Napster take root first, have already moved ahead with their own legal service, Movielink (www.movielink.com).

Let us now ask what the movie and music industries would do if copyright protection were far weaker, so that a buyer of a CD or DVD could, fairly easily, give copies to friends or even sell them cheaply to strangers. One possibility is that studios would just scale back their operations: fewer artists or movies would be profitable. Another possibility is that the industry would pursue technological copy protection, for instance selling disks that need a one-time complementary digital "key" to function, especially if a strong DRM system could prevent users from copying the protected work in a less secure form. A third possibility would be to revert to "public performances" (presumably with camcorders banned from the theaters) as the major revenue source. A common theme is that one might expect those who control content to hold the content more closely if they become less able to let it out without losing control over it completely.

A very different alternative is to put the content out there at a nominal (or no) charge and to earn revenues through sales of complements. For instance, a firm might offer content (software) for free, but ensure that it can be played only on that firm's proprietary hardware (and charge a mark-up on the latter). Of course, something would have to prevent copying of the hardware, but at least hardware is not subject to costless reproduction and distribution using digital technology. Such a strategy might seem to require consumers to own half a dozen separate CD players, clearly an unacceptable alternative, but this could be avoided by using a generic CD player along with suitable "keys" that would let that player play music from the various labels, rather as the authorization information is encoded in the SIM in a GSM phone. If the key were temporary, this would work similarly to a subscription TV service. Hardware manufacturers might even bundle multiple keys, in the limit effectively funding the software industry by something close to a tax on hardware. In Britain, the BBC is funded by a (government-enforced) tax on owning a TV set. Clearly, the legal and technical aspects of DRM systems become quite important in these scenarios.[35] An alternative complements strategy is to bundle the music, or video content, with advertisements. This is already happening in television shows, where "product placement" is becoming more important.

16 Switching costs and lock-in

Intellectual property rights greatly influence the switching costs associated with information technology such as computer hardware and software. A leading example is Microsoft Office. In addition to the user interfaces associated with Microsoft Word, Excel, and PowerPoint, with which millions of users have become familiar, these software programs involve proprietary file formats that have trade secret and copyright protection. File formats are an important aspect of switching costs: a major obstacle facing other productivity programs is the difficulty they have achieving full compatibility when importing and exporting files from and to Microsoft Office. For example, Sun's StarOffice has had trouble

---

[35] For one view of DRM, see Samuelson (2003).

offering good enough compatibility to take significant sales away from Microsoft Office.

To illustrate how property rights can affect switching costs, consider "number portability." Only in late 2003 did the Federal Communications Commission finally require wireless phone companies to let customers keep their phone numbers when switching carriers; the analogous requirement for "ordinary" phones was part of the 1996 Telecommunications Act, and its implementation was made a precondition for Bell companies to provide long-distance service in-region. Number portability makes it less painful for customers to switch carriers, and thus has a direct beneficial effect on consumers. However, precisely because number portability limits the ability of carriers to earn profit margins from their existing customers, number portability also weakens competition for new customers. Theory suggests that this effect could sometimes dominate the first effect, so that portability could in principle weaken rather than strengthen overall competition, i.e. harm rather than benefit customers. In practice, however, most informed commentators seem confident that number portability will increase competition and reduce prices.[36] There is no immediate prospect for "email address portability," and most people must still change their email address when they change ISP (or employer). Similar issues arise when customers want to take "their" data to a new provider, as when a patient wants to take medical or dental records to a new doctor or dentist, or even when a customer wants to take his or her purchase history data to a new online supplier of groceries or books.

While many economists often think of markets with switching costs as involving repeated purchases of the same good, an equally important pattern is the sale of a "primary" good in a "foremarket" followed by purchases of a complementary "secondary" product in an "aftermarket." In these situations, there can be switching costs if the seller of the primary good has an advantage in selling the complement. A classic example involves the sale of a piece of durable equipment, such as a photocopier, followed by aftermarket sales of parts and service for that equipment. Clearly, the

---

[36] See, for example, Viard (2003).

equipment manufacturer has an advantage in selling spare parts for its own machine, especially if such parts are patented or manufactured subject to significant economies of scale. Another example involves the licensing of complex business software, such as database software or transaction processing software, followed by annual upgrades and support for that software. Again, the initial vendor is very likely to have a significant advantage over third-party vendors in providing both upgrades and support for its software.[37] In some cases, the "aftermarket" occurs immediately after the foremarket transaction. Familiar examples include telephone service from a hotel room or even food at a sporting event. Casual empiricism indicates that the prices of these complementary goods and services are well above the levels that prevail when customers face more instantaneous options.

These "secondary markets" have been controversial. The *Kodak* antitrust case received widespread attention because it had been remanded back from the Supreme Court (which had ruled that competition faced by Kodak from Xerox in the foremarket did not *necessarily* imply that Kodak lacked market power in the aftermarkets for Kodak parts and service) and because Kodak ultimately was required by the Ninth Circuit to sell its patented parts to third-party service organizations who sought to service Kodak equipment.[38] But the *Kodak* case appears to be an anomaly in imposing a duty to deal on a patent holder. Indeed, in a more recent case involving Xerox, the Federal Circuit came to precisely the opposite conclusion.[39] A comparison of the two cases is peculiar, in that very similar practices were at issue, involving the same basic products (photocopiers), and Xerox had a far stronger position in the photocopier market, but the duty to deal was only imposed upon Kodak. One explanation, albeit not a very satisfying one, is that Xerox stressed its patent claims more strongly

---

[37] As one of us has emphasized in previous writings, in many cases customers purchase such products based on the total cost of ownership, and effective competition takes place in the foremarket, where prices may be discounted in recognition that margins will be earned in the aftermarket.

[38] *Image Technical Services* vs. *Eastman Kodak Company*, 125 F.3rd 1195 (Ninth Circuit, 1997). Shapiro served as an expert witness for Kodak in this case.

[39] Independent Service Organizations Antitrust Litigation, 203 F.3rd 1322 (Federal Circuit, 2000).

and earlier than did Kodak, so that the Xerox case was heard on appeal in the Federal Circuit, which arguably is more deferential to the rights of patent holders than is the Ninth Circuit. Very recently, the Supreme Court has made it clear that even monopolists will not generally be faced with a duty to help out their competitors,[40] although of course this does not mean that owners of intellectual property have a "free pass" against antitrust law.[41] In a separate intellectual property case, Lexmark (which produces printers) sued Static Control Components for violations of intellectual property when SSC reverse-engineered Lexmark's printer-cartridge interface, which Lexmark had made proprietary presumably in order to be able to mark up its aftermarket cartridges.[42]

17 Standards and patents

Patent rights can be central as firms negotiate compatibility and interface standards. Examples include the various standards by which modems communicate, the DVD read and write standards, and the MPEG standard for coding audio-visual information in a compressed digital format. As Professor Varian notes, many standard-setting organizations require participants to disclose all relevant intellectual property rights and agree to license any essential patents on "fair, reasonable, and non-discriminatory" terms.[43] Unfortunately, these rules have regularly led to disputes over the extent of the disclosure obligation, the scope of the licensing commitment, and what constitute "fair, reasonable and non-discriminatory" licensing terms.

---

[40] *Verizon Communications* vs. *Law Offices of Curtis V. Trinko*, decided 13 January 2004.

[41] Thus Microsoft argued, on appeal, that "if intellectual property rights have been lawfully acquired," then "their subsequent exercise cannot give rise to antitrust liability." The court dismissed this as "no more correct than the proposition that use of one's personal property, such as a baseball bat, cannot give rise to tort liability."

[42] *Lexmark International* vs. *Static Control Components, Inc.*, Civil Action 02-571-KSF.

[43] For an extensive discussion of how different standard-setting organizations treat intellectual property rights, see Lemley (2002).

The essence of the problem is that the power enjoyed by a patent holder whose technology is embodied in a standard can be far greater after the standard is widely adopted than at the earlier point in time when various alternative specifications were under consideration for the standard, some of which did not rely on the patented technology. If the participants in the standard-setting organization are aware of the relevant patent(s) early on, they can pick an alternative specification that does not infringe on the patent or they can negotiate acceptable licensing terms with the patent holder(s), perhaps even a royalty-free license. Once a standard is adopted that requires use of the patent, however, the bargaining power shifts, perhaps markedly, towards the patent holder. In other words, hold-up can develop if an industry adopts a technology as a standard and that technology later is found to infringe on a single firm's patent. The resulting *ex post* market power of the patent holder can be very substantial, especially if participants are locked in to the chosen standard through network effects as well as through ordinary sunk costs. The result is that the patent holder may be able to extract significantly more than the "true" or underlying value of its intellectual property, which is normally best measured by adopters' willingness to pay for it when they know their alternatives and have not yet made investments specific to that technology.

This problem has fueled a number of disputes, several of which led to lawsuits.[44] An example is the FTC's complaint against Rambus.[45] According to the FTC, Rambus concealed from a standards organization, JEDEC, its pending patent claims for dynamic random access memory (DRAM), which it was meanwhile amending based on information from JEDEC meetings. The result was that JEDEC memory standards (allegedly) infringed on Rambus's subsequently issued patents. This is not the first case

---

[44] Both authors have served as consultants to the parties in some of these matters.
[45] In the *Matter of Rambus, Inc.*, FTC Docket No. 9302. As of this writing, the FTC Administrative Law Judge had issued an opinion dismissing the FTC's complaint against Rambus in this matter. See http://www.ftc.gov/ os/adjpro/d9302/040223initialdecision.pdf. This decision has been appealed to the Commission. A related private case was decided by the Federal Circuit in favor of Rambus. See *Rambus Inc. vs. Infineon Technologies*, decided 29 January 2003.

with allegations of strategic hold-up. For example, Wang sued Mitsubishi for infringing patents on a memory module design that Wang had encouraged JEDEC[46] and the industry to adopt without disclosing its pending patents; the FTC later settled a somewhat similar matter with Dell in connection with the VESA bus. Rockwell and Motorola earlier had a dispute over Motorola's patents involving modem standards. These cases share the feature that a patent-holder's conduct allegedly created or worsened information and negotiation problems, exacerbating hold-up.

We do not mean to suggest that patents always present problems in the context of standards. On the contrary, there are many examples where participants have agreed to contribute their patents on a royalty-free or low-royalty basis to a specification that becomes a new and successful standard. A good example of this happy fact pattern is that of the Universal Serial Bus (USB), promoted by Intel.[47] The USB licensing terms require that companies making USB-compliant devices agree not to assert any patents they may have that are essential to compliance with the USB standard against others for manufacturing their own USB-compliant devices. Because of its strong position in a complement (microprocessors), Intel has incentives to make USB a successful, widely used product, suggesting that Intel judges that this weakening of intellectual property will improve the product's prospects. To be sure, Intel could also have less salutary incentives,[48] but we note that it did not succumb to the temptation (if any) to make USB unavailable on Apple or AMD-based machines.

18 Do we need to reform the patent system?

More and more observers are calling for reform to the US patent system. The fundamental problem identified by these observers is that of patent quality: too many "questionable" patents are issued

---

[46] The JEDEC Solid State Technology Association, formerly known as the Joint Electron Device Engineering Council.

[47] Shapiro served as an expert witness for Intel in one case involving the USB specification.

[48] On complementors' incentives, see, e.g., Farrell and Weiser (2003).

by the Patent and Trademark Office (PTO), i.e. patents are granted to companies or individuals who have not made genuine inventions, or patents are granted with overly broad claims. According to this view, the PTO has failed to understand or appreciate "prior art" in many cases and has awarded patents for inventions that did not in fact meet the novelty and non-obviousness requirements of patent law. Such "questionable" patents harm competition and innovation by imposing an unnecessary, unjustified, and costly burden on those companies or industries that are forced to either invent around these patents, pay royalties, or engage in costly and risky litigation.

Critics see these problems as especially severe in industries in which: (1) a large number of patents are being issued; (2) innovation is cumulative with a steady stream of incremental improvements, many of which should not in fact meet the non-obviousness requirement; (3) the Patent and Trademark Office has a relatively poor understanding of the technical literature and the underlying technology, and thus has frequently failed to take proper note of prior art; (4) a single product may potentially infringe on many patents, so products may be forced to pay royalties to multiple patent holders, a situation known as "royalty stacking;" or (5) manufacturers make sunk investments to bring products to market and may be held up by patents issued after these investments have been made. The semiconductor and software industries are usually thought to meet several of these criteria, and thus be most harmed by "questionable" patents.[49]

A recent and influential report by the Federal Trade Commission (2003) contains several important proposals for reform.[50] The FTC report finds that "questionable patents are a significant competitive concern and can harm innovation." As the term is used in the FTC report, "A poor quality or questionable patent is one that is likely invalid or contains claims that are likely overly broad" (p. 5). Several key FTC recommendations are designed to reduce

[49] See, for example, Merges (1999); Shapiro (2001b); Lemley (2001); and Cohen and Merrill (2004).
[50] In April 2004, the National Research Council released its own report evaluating the patent system and suggesting reforms; National Research Council (2004). Many critics of the current patent system are hopeful that these two reports will help galvanize support for legislative changes in the patent system.

harm to competition and innovation associated with questionable patents.[51]

According to the FTC, one reason too many questionable patents are issued is that existing means of challenging (issued or prospective) patents are inadequate. Third parties cannot challenge issued patents unless the patent owner has threatened the potential challenger with patent infringement litigation; and the patent enjoys a strong presumption of validity in any such court challenge. Moreover, if a challenger's rivals also would gain from the overturning of a "questionable" patent, the incentives for one firm to challenge may be quite weak. The FTC's first recommendation calls for legislation to create a new administrative procedure for post-grant review of and opposition to patents. The second recommendation calls for legislation to specify that challenges to the validity of a patent are to be determined based on a "preponderance of the evidence" rather than the current "clear and convincing evidence" standard of proof. This change has some merit given that the PTO issues many patents based on a rather quick review and with incomplete understanding of the underlying technology or prior art, although it would create greater uncertainty regarding patent rights generally.[52]

The FTC has additional recommendations to improve patent quality. Its third recommendation seeks to tighten the legal standard used to evaluate whether a patent is "obvious" while its fourth seeks additional funding for the PTO.

We also note here the FTC's seventh recommendation, which calls for legislation requiring the publication of all patent applications eighteen months after filing. Until recently, patents were published only when issued. This created significant problems with opportunism and lock-in. As the FTC explains, "During the time that would pass between the filing of a patent application and the issuance of a patent, an applicant's competitors could have invested substantially in designing and developing a product

---

[51] For a more complete discussion of the FTC's patent reform proposals, see Shapiro (2004) and Samuelson (2004).

[52] For an analysis of the limitations of post-grant opposition procedures and litigation as a method of promoting competition and innovation by invalidating patents that were improperly issued, see Farrell and Merges (2004).

and bringing it to market, only to learn, once the patent finally issued, that it was infringing a rival's patent and owed significant royalties. This scenario disrupts business planning and can reduce incentives to innovate and discourage competition." We agree, adding that this scenario can harm innovation and competition even if the patent holder and the firm developing and bringing the new product to market are not rivals.

Such problems are significantly reduced now that most patent applications are published eighteen months after filing; the exception is applications that are filed only in the US. The FTC would further reduce the problem by removing this exception. The FTC's eighth recommendation would further alleviate problems of hold-up by establishing certain prior user rights for companies that independently discover and implement technologies that are subsequently patented.

19 Summary and conclusions

Intellectual property – copyrights, patents, and trade secrets – promises to play an increasingly important role in the economy of the 21st century as information and information technology comprise a greater and greater proportion of economic activity. We have explained here some of the key ways in which intellectual property rights are granted and used in competitive strategy. Not surprisingly, copyright law and patent law are under pressure to evolve as information technology advances so rapidly.

Copyright law is critical in the information content industries, including publishing, music, movies, and computer software. The courts are currently working through the proper interpretation and role of copyright law and policy in the digital age. New technologies, many fitting under the rubric of "Digital Rights Management," can be used by rights holders to restrict what would otherwise be the fair use of copyright works. Few expect rapid resolution of the battle between those who see the Internet as a great intellectual commons where "information wants to be free" and those who see the Internet as a giant illegal machine for unauthorized reproduction of copyrighted works.

Likewise, patent law and policy are under pressure as the number of patents grows rapidly in the information technology sector of the economy. Many observers are deeply concerned that the patent system is out of balance, with the Patent and Trademark Office issuing many "questionable" patents and thereby harming competition and innovation. Here, the battle between those who benefit from the current system, with its arguably lax standards for the issuance of patents, and those who bear the costs of those patents, also is heating up rather than winding down. In the near future, there is a real prospect that the US patent system will be reformed to reduce the number of "questionable" patents, perhaps along the lines suggested in the Federal Trade Commission's 2003 report.

Bibliography

Alessandro Acquisti and Hal R. Varian, 2001. Conditioning prices on purchase history. Technical report, School of Information Management, University of California at Berkeley

William James Adams and Janet L. Yellen, 1976. Commodity bundling and the burden of monopoly. *Quarterly Journal of Economics*, 90 (3): 475–498

Mark Armstrong, 1999. Price discrimination by a many-product firm. *Review of Economic Studies*, 66 (1): 151–168

Mark Armstrong and John Vickers, 2001. Competitive price discrimination. *RAND Journal of Economics*, 32 (4): 579–605; http://www.nuff.ox.ac.uk/economics/people/armstrong/markpapers.html

Lawrence M. Ausubel, 1991. The failure of competition in the credit card market. *American Economic Review*, 81 (1): 50–81

Charles Babcock, 2001. Will open source get snagged in .NET? *ZDNet News*, 6 August; http://www.zdnet.com/zdnn/stories/news/0,4586,2801560,00.html

Mark Bagnoli and Ted Bergstrom, 1989. Log-concave probability and its application. Unpublished working paper; http://www.econ.ucsb.edu/~tedb/Theory/delta.pdf

G. Baker and T. Hubbard, 2000. Contractibility and asset ownership: Computers and governance in the US trucking industry. Technical Report 7634, National Bureau of Economic Research

Yannis Bakos and Erik Brynjolfsson, 1999. Bundling information goods: Pricing, profits and efficiency. *Management Science*, 45 (12): 1613–1630

2000. Bundling and competition on the Internet: Aggregation strategies for information goods. *Marketing Science*, 19 (1): 63–82; http://ebusiness.mit.edu/erik/

2001. Aggregation and disaggregation of information goods: Implications for bundling, site licensing and micropayment systems. In Brian Kahin and Hal R. Varian, eds., *Internet Publishing and Beyond: The Economics of Digital Information and Intellectual Property*. MIT Press, Cambridge, MA; http://ebusiness.mit.edu/erik/

M. Baye and John Morgan, 2001. Price dispersion in the lab and on the Internet: Theory and evidence. Technical report, Woodrow Wilson School, Princeton University; http://www.princeton.edu/~rjmorgan/working.htm

M. Baye, J. Morgan, and P. Scholten, 2001. Price dispersion in the small and in the large: Evidence from an Internet price comparison site. Technical report, Woodrow Wilson School, Princeton University; http://www.princeton.edu/~rjmorgan/working.htm

Alan Beggs and Paul Klemperer, 1992. Multi-period competition with switching costs. *Econometrica*, 60 (3): 651–666

Stanley Besen and Joseph Farrell, 1994. Choosing how to compete: Strategies and tactics in standardization. *Journal of Economic Perspectives*, 8 (2): 117–131

Robert Boynton, 2004. The tyranny of copyright. *New York Times Magazine*, 25 January

Adam M. Brandenburger and Barry J. Nalebuff, 1996. *Co-opetition*. Doubleday, New York

Timothy Bresnahan and M. Trajtenberg, 1995. General Purpose Technologies: Engines of growth? *Journal of Econometrics*, 65 (1): 83–108

Gerald Brock, 1981. *The Telecommunications Industry: The Dynamics of Market Structure*. Harvard University Press, Cambridge, MA

Erik Brynjolfsson and Lorin M. Hitt, 2000. Beyond computation: Information technology, organizational transformation and business performance. *Journal of Economic Perspectives*, 14 (4): 23–48

Erik Brynjolfsson and Michael Smith, 1999. Frictionless commerce? A comparison of Internet and conventional retailers. *Management Science*, 46 (4): 563–585; http://ebusiness.mit.edu/erik/

Nicholas G. Carr, 2003. IT doesn't matter. *Harvard Business Review*, May. 2004. *Does IT Matter?* Harvard Business School Press, Boston

Pei-Yu (Sharon) Chen and Lorin M. Hitt, 2001. Measuring the determinants of switching costs: A study of the on-line brokerage industry. Technical report, Wharton School

Clayton Christensen, 1997. *The Innovator's Dilemma: When New Technologies Cause Great Firms to Fail.* Harvard Business School Press, Boston

Ronald Coase, 1937. The nature of the firm. *Economica,* 4: 386–405

1972. Durability and monopoly. *Journal of Law and Economics,* 15 (1): 143–149.

Wesley M. Cohen and Stephen A. Merrill, eds., 2004. *Patents in the Knowledge Based Economy,* Committee on Intellectual Property Rights in the Knowledge-Based Economy, Board on Science, Technology, and Economic Policy, Policy and Global Affairs, National Research Council of the National Academies of Science, The National Academies Press, Washington, DC

Wesley Cohen, Richard Nelson, and John Walsh, 2000. Protecting their intellectual assets: Appropriability conditions and why US manufacturing firms patent (or not). National Bureau of Economic Research Working Paper 7552

Augustin Cournot, 1838. *Recherches sur les principes mathématiques de la théorie des richesses.* Hachette, Paris

Alan Cowell, 2001. Profit soars at SAP. *New York Times,* 20 July

J. Dana and K. Spier, 2000. Revenue sharing, demand uncertainty, and control of competing firms. Technical report, Northwestern University

Paul A. David, 1990. The dynamo and the computer: An historical perspective on the modern productivity paradox. *American Economic Review,* 80: 355–361

J. Bradford Delong and A. Michael Froomkin, 2001. Speculative microeconomics for tomorrow's economy. In Brian Kahin and Hal R. Varian, eds., *Internet Publishing and Beyond: The Economics of Digital Information and Intellectual Property.* MIT Press, Cambridge, MA; http://www.j-bradford-delong.net/OpEd/virtual/technet/spmicro.html

Raymond Deneckere and Preston McAfee, 1996. Damaged goods. *Journal of Economics and Management Strategy,* 5 (2): 149–174

David Dranove and Neil Gandal, 2000. The DVD vs. DIVX standard war: Empirical evidence of vaporware. Technical Report CPC00–16, University of California at Berkeley

Phred Dvorak, Nick Wingfield, and Sarah McBride, 2004. Technology titans battle over format of DVD successor. *Wall Street Journal,* 15 March

Nicholas Economides, 1996. The economics of networks. *International Journal of Industrial Organization*, 16 (4): 673–699; http://raven. stern.nyu.edu/networks/

Nicholas Economides and Charles Himmelberg, 1995. Critical mass and network size with application to the US fax market. Technical report, Stern School of Business, New York University; http://raven.stern. nyu.edu/networks/papers.html

Glenn Ellison and Sara Fisher Ellison, 2001. Search, obfuscation, and price elasticities on the Internet. Technical report, Department of Economics, MIT

Joseph Farrell and Paul Klemperer, 2003. Coordination and lock-in: Competition with switching costs and network effects. In Mark Armstrong and Rob Porter, eds., *Handbook of Industrial Organization*, vol. III. Amsterdam, North-Holland; http://www.paulklemperer.org

Joseph Farrell and Robert Merges 2004. Incentives to challenge and defend patents. *Berkeley Technology Law Journal*, forthcoming

Joseph Farrell and Garth Saloner, 1992. Converters, compatibility, and the control of interfaces. *Journal of Industrial Economics*, March: 9–35

Joseph Farrell and Carl Shapiro, 1988. Dynamic competition with switching costs. *Rand Journal of Economics*, 19: 123–137

    1989. Optimal contracts with lock-in. *American Economic Review*, 79 (1): 51–68

Joseph Farrell and Philip J. Weiser, 2003. Modularity, vertical integration, and open access policies: Towards a convergence of antitrust and regulation in the internet age. *Harvard Journal of Law and Technology*, 17 (1): 85–135

Federal Trade Commission, 2003. To promote innovation: The proper balance of competition and patent law and policy; http://www.ftc.gov/opa/2003/10/cpreport.htm

Drew Fudenberg and Jean Tirole, 1985. Preemption and rent equalization in the adoption of new technology. *Review of Economic Studies*, 52: 383–402

    1987. Understanding rent dissipation: On the uses of game theory in industrial organization. *American Economic Review Papers and Proceedings*, 77: 176–183

    1998. Upgrades, trade-ins, and buy-backs. *Rand Journal of Economics*, 29: 238–258

    2000. Customer poaching and brand switching. *Rand Journal of Economics*, 31: 634–657

Nancy Gallini, 2002. The economics of patents: Lessons from recent US patent reform. *Journal of Economic Perspectives*, 16 (2): 131–154

Nancy Gallini and Suzanne Scotchmer, 2001. Intellectual property: When is it the best incentive system? In Adam Jaffe, Joshua Lerner, and Scott Stern, eds., *Innovation Policy and the Economy*, vol. II. MIT Press, Cambridge, MA

Richard J. Gilbert and Michael L. Katz, 2001. An economist's guide to *US v. Microsoft*. *Journal of Economic Perspectives*, 15 (2): 25–44

S. Colum Gilfillan, 1935. *Inventing the Ship*. Follett, Chicago

Austan Goolsbee and Peter J. Klenow, 2000. Evidence on learning and network externalities in the diffusion of home computers. Technical report, University of Chicago; http://gsbadg.uchicago.edu/vitae.htm

Robert J. Gordon, 2000. Does the "New Economy" measure up to the great inventions of the past? *Journal of Economic Perspectives*, 14 (4): 49–74

Amy R. Greenwald and Jeffrey O. Kephart, 1999. Shopbots and pricebots. Technical report, IBM Watson Labs; http://www.research.ibm.com/infoecon/paps/html/amec99_shopbot/ shopbot.html

Ward Hanson, 1998. The original WWW: Web lessons from the early days of radio. *Journal of Interactive Marketing*, 12 (3): 46–56; http://www3.interscience.wiley.com/cgi-bin/issuetoc?ID=79208

E. Helpman, 1998. *General Purpose Technologies and Economic Growth*. MIT Press, Cambridge, MA

Arye Hillman and John G. Riley, 1989. Politically contestable rents and transfers. *Economics and Politics*, 1: 17–39

David A. Hounshell, 1984. *From the American System to Mass Production, 1800–1932*. Johns Hopkins University Press, Baltimore

Thomas N. Hubbard, 2000. The demand for monitoring technologies. *Quarterly Journal of Economics*, May: 533–560

Maarten C. W. Janssen and José Luis Moraga-González, 2001. Two firms is enough for competition, but three or more is better. Technical report, Rotterdam University

Matthew Josephson, 1959. *Edison: A Biography*. McGraw-Hill, New York

Michael L. Katz and Carl Shapiro, 1985. Network externalities, competition, and compatibility. *American Economic Review*, 75 (3): 424–440

1986a. Product compatibility choice in a market with technological progress. *Oxford Economic Papers*, 38 (Special Issue on the New Industrial Economics): 146–165

1986b. Technology adoption in the presence of network externalities. *Journal of Political Economy*, 94 (4): 822–884

1992. Product introduction with network externalities. *Journal of Industrial Economics*, 40: 55–84

1994. Systems competition and network effects. *Journal of Economic Perspectives*, 8 (2): 93–115

Stuart Kauffman, 1995. *At Home in the Universe: The Search for the Laws of Self-Organization and Complexity.* Oxford University Press, Oxford

Moshe Kim, Doron Kliger, and Bent Vale, 2003. Estimating switching costs: The case of banking. *Journal of Financial Intermediation*, 12 (1): 25–56

Benjamin Klein, 2001. The Microsoft case: What can a dominant firm do to defend its market position? *Journal of Economic Perspectives*, 15 (2): 45–62

Paul Klemperer, 1987. Markets with consumer switching costs. *Quarterly Journal of Economics*, 102 (2): 375–394

1989. Price wars caused by switching costs. *Review of Economic Studies*, 56 (3): 405–420

1995. Competition when consumers have switching costs: An overview with applications to industrial organization, macroeconomics and international trade. *Review of Economic Studies*, 62: 515–539; http://www.paulklemperer.org/index.htm

S. Kortum and J. Lerner, 1998. Stronger protection or technological revolution: What is behind the recent surge in patenting? *Carnegie-Rochester Conference Series on Public Policy*, 48: 247–304

Alex Kuczynski, 2001. Big magazines get bigger as small ones get gobbled up. *New York Times*, 30 July; http://www.nytimes.com/2001/07/30/business/30MAG.html?pagewanted=print

S. J. Leibowitz and Stephen Margolis, 1990. The fable of the keys. *Journal of Law and Economics*, 33: 1–26

Mark Lemley, 2001. Rational ignorance at the patent office. *Northwestern University Law Review*, 95: 1495–1532; http://repositories.cdlib.org/blewp/19

2002. Intellectual property rights and standard-setting organization. *California Law Review*, 90: 1889–1980; available at www.ssrn.com

Lawrence Lessig, 2001. *The Future of Ideas: The Fate of the Commons in a Connected World.* Random House, New York

R. Levin, A. Klevorick, R. Nelson, and S. Winter, 1987. "Appropriating the returns from industrial R&D," *Brookings Papers on Economic Activity*, 3: 783–820

Martin Libicki, James Schneider, Dave R. Frelinger, and Ann Slomovic, 2000. *Scaffolding the New Web: Standards and Standards Policy for the Digital Economy.* RAND, Santa Monica; http://www.rand.org/publications/MR/MR1215/

Robert Litan and Alice Rivlin, 2001. *The Economic Payoff from the Internet Revolution.* Brookings Institution Press, Washington, DC

Robert Litan and Hal Varian, 2001. The netimpact study. Technical report, University of California at Berkeley, http://www.netimpactstudy.com

Gregory Mankiw and Michael Whinston, 1986. Free entry and social inefficiency. *Rand Journal of Economics*, 17 (1): 48–58

Charles Mann, 1998. Who will own your next good idea? *The Atlantic Online*, September; http://www.theatlantic.com/issues/98sep/copy.htm

Peter Menell, 2000. Intellectual property: General theories. In Boudewijn Bouckaert and Gerrit de Gees, eds., *Encyclopedia of Law and Economics*. Edward Elgar, Cheltenham

2003. Envisioning copyright law's digital future. *New York Law School Law Review*, 46: 63–109

Robert Merges, 1999. As many as six impossible patents before breakfast: property rights for business concepts and patent system reform. *Berkeley Technology Law Journal*, 14 (2): 577–615

Judith Holland Mortimer, 2001. The effects of revenue-sharing contracts on welfare in vertically separated markets: Evidence from the video rental industry. Technical report, Economics Department, Harvard University

Barry Nalebuff, 1999. Bundling. Technical Report 99–14, School of Management, Yale University

2000. Competing against bundles. Technical Report 00–7, School of Management, Yale University

National Research Council, 2004. *A Patent System for the 21st Century*, ed. Stephen A. Merrill, Richard C. Levin, and Mark B. Myers. Committee on Intellectual Property Rights in the Knowledge-Based Economy, Board on Science, Technology, and Economic Policy, Policy and Global Affairs, National Research Council of the National Academies of Science, Washington, DC

Waltern Oi, 1971. A Disneyland dilemma: Two-part tariffs for a Mickey Mouse monopoly. *Quarterly Journal of Economics*, 85: 77–96

Jennifer Reinganum, 1989. The timing of innovation: Research, development, and diffusion. In R. Schmalensee and R. Willig, eds., *Handbook of Industrial Organization*. North-Holland, Amsterdam

John G. Riley, 1999. Asymmetric contests: A resolution of the Tullock paradox. In Peter Howitt, Elisabetta De Antoni, and Axel Leijonhufvud, eds., *Money, Markets and Method: Essays in Honor of Robert W. Clower*. Edward Elgar, Cheltenham; http://www.econ.ucla.edu/riley/research/

Jeffrey Rohlfs, 1974. A theory of interdependent demand for a communications service. *Bell Journal of Economics*, 5 (1): 16–37

2001. *Bandwagon Effects in High-Technology Industries.* MIT Press, Cambridge, MA

Monica Roman, 2001. Black ink all over Hewlett-Packard. *Business Week,* 22 January; http://www.businessweek.com/@@8zC3j2QQgISnLgEA/premium/content/ 01_22/

Linda Rosencrance, 2000. Amazon charging different prices on some DVDs. *Computerworld,* 5 September; http://www.computerworld.com/cwi/story/0,1199,NAV47_STO49569,00.html

Stephen W. Salant, 1989. When is inducing self-selection suboptimal for a monopolist? *Quarterly Journal of Economics,* 104 (2): 391–397

Pamela Samuelson, 2003. DRM {and, or, vs.} the law. *Communications of the ACM,* April: 41–45; http://www.sims.berkeley.edu/~pam/papers.html

2004. Legally speaking: Why reform the US patent system? Unpublished paper; http://www.sims.berkeley.edu/~pam/papers.html

Pamela Samuelson and Suzanne Scotchmer, 2002. The law and economics of reverse engineering. *Yale Law Journal,* 111: 1575–1663

Pamela Samuelson and Hal R. Varian, 2002. The "New Economy" and information technology policy. In Jeffrey Frankle, ed., *Economic Policy During the Clinton Administration.* MIT Press, Cambridge, MA; http://www.sims.berkeley.edu/~hal

Richard Schmalensee, 1981a. Monopolistic two-part tariff arrangements. *Bell Journal of Economics,* 12: 445–466

1981b. Output and welfare implications of monopolistic third-degree price discrimination. *American Economic Review,* 71: 242–247

Joseph Schumpeter, 1934. *The Theory of Economic Development.* Harvard University Press, Cambridge, MA

2000. The analysis of economic change. In Richard V. Clemence, ed., *Essays on Entrepreneurs, Innovations, Business Cycles and the Evolution of Capitalism.* Transaction Books, New Brunswick, pp. 134–149. Originally published in *Review of Economic Statistics,* May 1935.

Carl Shapiro, 2000. Competition policy in the information economy. In Einar Hope, ed., *Foundations of Competition Policy Analysis,* vol. XXV. Routledge, New York

2001a. Cross licenses, patent pools, and standard-setting. In Adam Jaffe, Joshua Lerner, and Scott Stern, eds., *Innovation Policy and the Economy,* vol. II. MIT Press, Cambridge, MA

2001b. Navigating the patent thicket. In Adam Jaffe, Joshua Lerner, and Scott Stern, eds., *Innovation Policy and the Economy,* National Bureau of Economics, Washington, DC; http://faculty.haas.berkeley.edu/shapiro

2004. Patent system reform: economic analysis and critique. *Berkeley Technology Law Journal*, forthcoming; http://faculty.haas.berkeley.edu/shapiro

Carl Shapiro and Hal R. Varian, 1998a. *Information Rules*. Harvard Business School Press, Cambridge, MA; http://www.inforules.com

1998b. Versioning: The smart way to sell information. *Harvard Business Review*, November–December: 106–114

Oz Shy, 2001. *The Economics of Network Industries*. Cambridge University Press, Cambridge

Susan Smulyan, 1994. *Selling Radio: The Commercialization of American Broadcasting*. Smithsonian Institution Press, Washington, DC

Charles Steindel and Kevin J. Stiroh, 2001. Productivity: What is it and why do we care? Technical report, New York Federal Reserve Bank; http://www.ny.frb.org/rmaghome/staffrp/2001/sr122.pdf

Kevin Stiroh, 2001. Information technology and the US productivity revival: What do the industry data say? Technical report, New York Federal Reserve Bank; http://www.ny.frb.org/rmaghome/staff_rp/2001/sr115.html

Nancy Stokey, 1979. Intertemporal price discrimination. *Quarterly Journal of Economics*, 93: 355–371

George V. Thompson, 1954. Intercompany technical standardization in the early American automobile industry. *Journal of Economic History*, 14 (1): 1–20

David Ulph and Nir Vulkan, 2000. Electronic commerce and competitive first-degree price discrimination. Technical report, University College, London; http://www.ecn.bris.ac.uk/www/ecnv/welcome.htm

David Ulph and Nir Vulkan, 2001. E-commerce, mass customization and price discrimination. Technical report, University College, London; http://www.ecn.bris.ac.uk/www/ecnv/welcome.htm

Abbott Usher, 1954. *A History of Mechanical Invention*. Dover, Cambridge, MA

Hal R. Varian, 1980. A model of sales. *American Economic Review*, 70: 651–659

1985. Price discrimination and social welfare. *American Economic Review*, 75 (4): 870–875

1997. Economic aspects of personal privacy. In Larry Irving, ed., *Privacy and Self-Regulation in the Information Age*. National Telecommunications and Information Administration, Washington, DC; http://www.ntia.doc.gov/reports/privacy/privacy_rpt.htm

2000. Buying, sharing and renting information goods. *Journal of Industrial Economics*, 48 (4): 473–488

2001. Versioning information goods. In Brian Kahin and Hal R. Varian, eds., *Internet Publishing and Beyond: The Economics of Digital Information and Intellectual Property*. MIT Press, Cambridge, MA; http://www.sims.berkeley.edu/~hal/people/hal/papers.html

Hal R. Varian and Carl Shapiro, 2003. Linux adoption in the public sector: An economic analysis. Unpublished paper; http://www.sims. berkeley.edu/~hal/Papers/2004/linux-adoption-in-the-public-sector.pdf

Brian Viard, 2003. Do switching costs make markets more or less competitive: The case of 800-number portability. Unpublished paper, Graduate School of Business, Stanford University; http://faculty-gsb.stanford.edu/viard/Personal/PDF/port.pdf

J. Miguel Villas-Boas, 1999. Dynamic competition with customer recognition. *RAND Journal of Economics*, 30 (4): 604–631

2001. Price cycles in markets with customer recognition. Technical report, Hass School of Business, University of California at Berkeley

Nir Vulkan, 2003. *The Economics of E-Commerce: A Strategic Guide to Understanding and Designing the Online Marketplace*. Princeton University Press, Princeton

Martin Weitzman, 1998. Recombinant growth. *Quarterly Journal of Economics*, 113: 331–360

Michael D. Whinston, 1990. Tying, foreclosure, and exclusion. *American Economic Review*, 80 (4): 837–859

2001. Exclusivity and tying in *US* v. *Microsoft*: What we know, and don't know. *Journal of Economic Perspectives*, 15 (2): 63–80

Index of names

Index of subjects